easy PEASY
All the Time

easy PeaSy All the Time

Real meals for kids who want to eat

Pru Irvine

EBURY PRESS
LONDON

This book is dedicated to all children who want to cook but especially to my mother who gave me my taste buds and a whole lot more.

First published in 2001

1 3 5 7 9 10 8 6 4 2

First published in the United Kingdom in 2001 by Ebury Press
Random House, 20 Vauxhall Bridge Road, London SW1V 2SA

www.randomhouse.co.uk

Random House Australia (Pty) Limited
20 Alfred Street, Milsons Point, Sydney,
New South Wales 2061, Australia

Random House New Zealand Limited
18 Poland Road, Glenfield, Auckland 10, New Zealand

Random House South Africa (Pty) Limited
Endulini, 5a Jubilee Road, Parktown 2193, South Africa

The Random House Group Limited Reg. No. 954009

Papers used by Ebury Press are natural, recyclable products made from wood grown in sustainable forests.

A CIP catalogue record for this book is available from the British Library.

ISBN 0 09 187782 2

Designed by Redpath
Edited by Nicky Thompson
Photography by Philip Webb and Craig Robertson
Food styling by Dagmar Vesely and Julie Beresford
Styling by Helen Trent

The publishers would like to thank Divertimenti (020 7581 8065) for the loan of all the kitchen equipment in this book.

Colour separation in Milan by Colorlito S.r.l.
Printed and bound in Portugal by Printer Portuguesa

Contents

6 **Dear Easy Peasies – Do you mix your peas with honey?**

8 **Inside Easy Peasy All the Time**

10 **Easy Peasy How to do Everything All the Time**

18 **Easy Peasy Helpful Tips**

19 **Easy Peasy Bits and Bobs**

21 **Laying the Table the Easy Peasy Way**

22 **Pots and Pans and Things**

26 **Wakey Wakey**

48 **Any Time**

88 **On the Table**

120 **How to Live Long Enough to Eat Your Next Meal**

124 **Only Cows Graze!**

125 **Index**

128 **Acknowledgements**

Dear Easy peasies

This book is for you and so is this quiz. The scores are at the end of the quiz, but don't look yet. The quiz is called:

Do you mix your peas with honey?

And all you have to do is tick the right box for you. Here goes.

1. Do you mix your peas with honey?
a) Yes ☐
b) No ☐
c) I'm not answering ☐

2. Do you ever eat ham for breakfast?
a) Yes ☐
b) No ☐
c) Don't be daft ☐

3. Do you eat breakfast?
a) Yes ☐
b) No ☐
c) Are you crazy? ☐

4. Do you ever go to school?
a) Yes ☐
b) No ☐
c) Not if I can help it ☐

5. Are you bored with your packed lunch box?
a) Yes ☐
b) No ☐
c) Sometimes ☐

6. Can you make your own packed lunch?
a) Yes ☐
b) No ☐
c) Ha! Ha! ☐

7. Do you make your own packed lunch?
a) Yes ☐
b) No ☐
c) Get lost ☐

8. Do you think you're going to win a prize for this quiz?
a) Yes ☐
b) No ☐
c) Is this a joke? ☐

9. Which is better for you?
a) Wholemeal bread ☐
b) White bread ☐
c) Don't know ☐

10. Do you ever eat fruit for a snack?
a) Yes ☐
b) No ☐
c) What's fruit? ☐

11. Can you tell the difference between salt and sugar?
a) Yes ☐
b) No ☐
c) What a stupid question ☐

12. Do you ever eat together as a family?
a) Yes ☐
b) No ☐
c) Sometimes ☐

13. Do you mostly enjoy your food?
a) Yes ☐
b) No ☐
c) Not interested ☐

14. Do you cook?
a) Yes ☐
b) No ☐
c) Where's the kitchen? ☐

15. Do you like junk food?
a) Yes ☐
b) No ☐
c) Get a life! ☐

16. If you were a cow would you eat?
a) Nearly all day ☐
b) Only in summer ☐
c) Only on Tuesdays ☐

17. Are you?
a) An animal ☐
b) A vegetable ☐
c) An alien ☐

Now work out your score.

If you ticked mostly As: You're a pretty smart cookie. You seem to know your peas from your honey. You deserve this book. If you keep going like this you're bound to grow up into an adult!

If you ticked mostly Bs: You've got a sense of humour, kid! You're going somewhere. Hopefully into the kitchen. You deserve this book. Once you've read it you could write your own!

If you ticked mostly Cs: I like your attitude – for an alien! You're obviously a happy-go-lucky-wise-cracking-smarty-pants. If you've ever thought of joining Planet Mankind then you deserve this book. What do aliens actually eat?

Love

Pru xxx

P.S. Hope you enjoy the book!

Inside Easy Peasy All the Time

You'll need about 1½ minutes to read this bit. So set your watch – GO!

Easy Peasy How to do Everything All the Time is your guide to doing each recipe with little or no adult help at all. Little, bite-sized chunks of useful information. How to skin a peach; how to separate eggs; how to tell manky food from fresh food; what is shredding? How will you know when something's cooked? What is a hand-held electric blender? All is revealed starting on page 10.

Pots and Pans and Things are pictures of all the utensils and equipment you will need to make everything in this book. Sometimes people call the same thing by a different name – my sieve might be your colander. So a picture helps everyone. Spot your colander starting on page 22.

Wakey Wakey is about getting up in the morning. Or wishing you didn't have to. Or letting someone else stay in bed while you make their breakfast for them.

Any Time is about weekends, school holidays, after school. good snacking and those times when you're supposed to be asleep but you're actually reading and eating a sandwich in bed.

On the Table is about getting stuck into those things called 'meals' for one person, for two people, for four people, for all of you. On the Table is about eating together.

How to Live Long Enough to Eat Your Next Meal is about not poisoning yourself or anyone else. Health and safety – BORING! But if you want to cook to eat and if you want to eat delicious things, you have to know how to avoid disaster in the kitchen.

Only Cows Graze! is about eating. Should we eat all day like cows do? Should we just eat in the summer and hibernate in the winter? Should we only ever eat breakfast, lunch and supper? All the answers are on page 124 – if you believe them!

Easy Peasy How to do Everything All the Time

Easy peasy ingredients

APPLES AND PEARS . . .

. . . often need peeling and coring if they're to be cooked. Use a sharp knife and a chopping board. **Cut** them from top to bottom and then into quarters. Using the knife, carefully cut out the hard core and the pips in the middle of each quarter and then carefully **peel** the fruit. It's best to peel pears and apples just before you need them because they go **brown** if they're left to hang around too long without their skins.

CARROTS . . .

. . . need peeling and washing. Use a sharp knife to take a slice off both ends. Hold the thick end of

the carrot with one hand and with the other, use a vegetable peeler to peel down from the top to the bottom. Keep turning until all the skin is gone. Then rinse the carrot in cold water.

Be careful **chopping** carrots. They're so hard that they have a way of sliding around. You can slice across into rounds or cut the carrot lengthways into two and then again into four, depending on the size.

EGGS . . .

. . . are great little things but some people are **allergic** to them. It's also not a good idea to eat **raw** egg if you're **very young, very old** or **pregnant**. **Cracking** eggs is one of those easy, difficult jobs. Put a small bowl on a steady surface. Give the shell a **bash** on the rim of the bowl. Now push both **thumbs** through the crack and let the egg fall into the bowl. If you bash it too hard, it'll run all over your fingers. A quick, firm whack and straight into the bowl. Just fish out any bits of shell that fall in.

Separating eggs is messy. You really need two **bowls** – one for the yolk and one for the white. Whack the egg quite hard in its middle over a bowl. Holding it upright in one hand, push your other **thumb** into the crack and gently prize apart the shell, keeping the yolk safely inside one half while the white **drips** into the bowl. Then, very gently, **tip** the yolk into the other side of the shell allowing more of the egg white to drip into the bowl. Keep doing this carefully until all the white has dripped off. You never get it all but you'll get most of it. Hard-boiling eggs is on page 14.

FRESH HERBS . . .

. . . need to be rinsed in cold water, given a good shaking and perhaps a pat dry in some kitchen paper. When you need a **'handful'**, it means just that – a handful. Squeeze the herbs you're using into a **ball** as best you can and cut them up on a chopping board using a sharp knife. When you've done that, gather all the bits together again and do the same thing until the herbs are chopped as small as you want them. Sometimes it's easier to cut them up with **scissors**. Have a go!

If you need to chop **woody** herbs like rosemary or thyme, it's often best to take off (and throw away) their woody stems and just chop the leaves.

If you're using fresh **garlic** that needs chopping, then use a sharp knife to cut a tiny slice off the top and bottom of the clove and then **peel** away the outer skin. There's no need to wash garlic. You can chop it in lots of ways – very thin slices or tiny chunks – or you can simply leave it whole. If you're using a **garlic crusher**, then just pop the clove in and squeeze until the juicy bits ooze out. You don't even have to peel it first.

FRESH ROOT GINGER . . .

. . . tastes quite **strong** so you only need to use a little at a time. Cut off a chunk the size you need and **scrub** it in cold, running water. Now slice it as thinly as you can with a sharp knife. If you don't want to wash it, then just **peel** it. Don't rub your eyes until you've washed your hands after slicing ginger, as it can sting.

LEEKS . . .

. . . can be very **muddy**. Think of them as giant spring onions when you're preparing them. Cut the messy green end off the leek and then take a slice off its white bottom. Now, using a sharp knife, **cut** down through the leek from top to bottom. Don't cut all the way through – just enough to show some of the inside. Using your fingers, **peel** away the outer layer of skin. The leek is now ready for some serious rinsing in cold water. Check the inside of the leek to be sure you've got rid of all the mud.

LEMONS . . .

. . . are **citrus** fruits (like oranges, limes and grapefruit). They always need **washing** in hot, **soapy** water to remove the wax from the skins. Remember to rinse them!

When you're asked to **zest** a lemon, it means peeling away tiny strips of the skin. You really need a zester for the job. Or you could try using a vegetable peeler and then carefully slicing the slithers very thinly with a sharp knife.

Lots of recipes need lemon juice and it's always the **pips** that get in the way. You can simply fish them out with clean fingers or a teaspoon. Better still, squeeze the lemon with a **lemon squeezer** and then pour the juice through a little sieve which will catch the pips.

MUSHROOMS . . .

. . . are usually pretty **dirty**. Wipe them clean with a piece of damp **kitchen paper**. Cut a thin slice off the stalk end and throw it away. Then slice or chop.

When you **fry** mushrooms you get a lot of **juice**. It's normally best to keep cooking them until the juice has gone.

ONIONS . . .

. . . always seem to need **peeling**. Take a sharp knife in one hand and hold the onion firmly with the other. **Slice** off the top and bottom and peel away the dry, papery skin. You may find it easier to cut the onion in half before peeling it. There's no need to wash onions after they've been peeled.

Slicing onions means cutting each one into quarters and then slicing across and down each quarter. Do this as thinly as you can manage. Any bits that fall away while you're cutting can just be chopped up at the end.

Chopping onions means cutting them into little chunks.

PEPPERS . . .

. . . usually need **chopping**. First **slice** off the stalk end and pull the pepper apart. Rinse out all the little white seeds under cold, running water and **pull** off any white bits of flesh. Now the pepper is ready for chopping or slicing or just eating raw.

POTATOES . . .

. . . need washing in cold water. To peel them, use a vegetable peeler. Hold the potato firmly in one hand and with the other hand **peel** from the top to the bottom of the potato, turning it around until there is no skin left. Peeled potatoes are **slippery** so be extra careful. If you're cooking jacket potatoes, don't peel them. Just scrub them and make sure they're completely **dry** before they go into the oven. If you're peeling potatoes before you need them, keep them covered in cold water. This stops them going brown.

RASPBERRIES AND STRAWBERRIES . . .

. . . need to be rinsed **gently** in cold, running water **just before** you use them. If you wash them and leave them they'll go mushy. When you're rinsing raspberries look out for little **insects** which like to hide inside. Throw away any mouldy fruit. The easiest way to take the stalk off a strawberry is to **slice** it off with a sharp knife. Throw away any yucky ones.

SALAD LEAVES . . .

. . . need washing before you eat them. If you buy ready-prepared, pre-washed bags from the supermarket, then all you have to do is open the bag and tip the salad into a bowl. If not then you need to **wash** salad leaves in cold, running water. Once you've got rid of any bits of mud, check for little **insects** – they like salad! Salad leaves need to be **dry** before you dress them. Either whizz them in a salad spinner if you've got one or dry them in some kitchen paper.

SALT . . .

. . . is quite tricky to get right. Too much salt is not good for you. Not enough salt often makes food seem dull. Sometimes food can taste quite different when you add salt. Use the quantities suggested in this book as a guide. Some of you like more salt than others. Experiment until you get it right for you. But try to use less salt not more.

SEASONED FLOUR . . .

. . . is nothing more than adding a **flavouring** like salt and pepper to flour before you cook with it. You might roll chunks of chicken or fish in seasoned flour, for example.

SPRING ONIONS . . .

. . . are like tiny leeks. To prepare a spring onion, cut off most of the dark green bits with a sharp knife. Then cut a **tiny** slice off the other end. Rinse it under cold water and pull away any loose bits. Now you can slice the onion in whichever way the recipe asks.

TOMATOES . . .

. . . are **fruits** that you can eat with most things. If you need to **skin** tomatoes, here's how: put them into a heatproof bowl and **stab** them a few times with a fork. Boil the kettle and carefully pour **boiling water** over them until they're just covered. Watch out for the hot steam. After a few minutes lift one tomato out with the **fork**. The skin should be **peeling** off. Just pull the rest off with your fingers. Remember they'll be hot, so you may have to let them cool a bit before skinning them.

WATER . . .

. . . from the tap should be used when you're washing foods. It must be cold water. Hot water should always come from a kettle that's been boiled. Hot water straight from the tap can be full of **nasty** things.

Easy peasy Know-how

BOILING . . .

. . . just means liquid that's been heated hot enough to **bubble** fast.

BROWNING . . .

. . . means just that – cooking **meat** over a high heat until it changes colour and starts to go a different shade of brown. When you're browning meat you need to keep stirring and turning it over with a wooden spoon. This stops it sticking to the bottom of the pan. You often find that a lot of juice comes out of the meat when you're browning it. It goes away eventually.

CARAMELISING . . .

. . . is simply **sugar** and **water** (or **sugar** and **fat**) that have been turned **light brown** by cooking over a high heat to make a **syrup**. You always need to watch something you're caramelising because the liquid can go from caramel to a **burnt**, sticky, dead saucepan in a matter of seconds. Caramelised liquids are also **very, very hot** so always be very careful. Keep the saucepan **handle** tucked in and make sure there is somewhere safe for you to put the pan when it comes off the heat.

COOKING VEGETABLES . . .

. . . is Easy Peasy if you remember a few things. Don't use much **water** and don't put **salt** in the water, unless you're cooking potatoes. Wait until you serve the vegetables before adding salt. Don't

cook them for too long. Serve them so they are a little **crunchy** and not a soggy mush. This way you'll manage to keep most of the natural goodness and **vitamins** in them.

FOLDING IN . . .

. . . means that instead of throwing or tipping something into a mixture, you carefully fold it – spoon by spoon of sugar into egg whites to make meringues, for example. Not whisking or stirring but gently **turning over** and mixing in.

FRYING . . .

. . . is hot work. It means cooking something in oil or butter that's hot enough to **sizzle**. Always use long-handled utensils because hot oil and butter can **spit** at you. Be careful. Frying is fast, **hot** cooking.

GRATING . . .

. . . is hard work on small hands. You can do it easily and quickly in the **food processor** using the grating attachment. If you do it by hand, hold the **grater** firmly in one hand, resting it on a board. With the other hand, **press** the food you're going to grate against the top of the grater and **slide** it up and down. Be careful not to skin your **knuckles** when you get close to the end. To protect your knuckles, it's often helpful to wrap a tea towel around the end of whatever you're grating.

GREASING . . .

. . . is a nice job. Lots of recipes need a greased tin, baking tray or dish. If you're using oil, simply pour a little into the dish and use a piece of **kitchen paper** to rub the oil all over the inside of the dish –

remember the **edges** and the **corners**. If you're using **butter**, take a blob of soft butter on a piece of kitchen paper and do the same. Greasing stops the food **sticking** to the dish so it's especially important to remember the corners. You can always use your **fingers** to do this job but wash them before and afterwards.

GRILLING . . .

. . . usually means using a grill with a grill pan and cooking food under an **overhead** heat. It's a good way of cooking with very little fat because grill pans are designed to let fat **drip** off the grilling rack and into the pan. But the grill pan gets really **mucky** and hard to clean. Try lining the grill pan with **kitchen foil** before you cook. That way the fat still drips through the rack but lands on the foil, so you can just scrumple it up and throw it away when you've finished. Let it cool down first.

HARD-BOILING AN EGG . . .

. . . is Easy Peasy. Put the egg in a saucepan with enough cold water to cover it. Bring it to the boil over a high heat and cook it for 7-8 minutes, depending how big it is (5-6 minutes for a small egg, longer for a big one). To check whether it's hard boiled, carefully lift the egg out of the saucepan with a spoon. If the water disappears quite quickly and leaves the shell looking dry, you'll know it's cooked. Carefully tip the hot water out of the saucepan into the sink. Put the egg back into the saucepan and run cold water over it to cool it down and stop it cooking. Leave the hard-boiled egg in the water until you need it, or let it get completely cold and then put it in the fridge.

KNEADING DOUGH . . .

. . . is great fun but requires **patience**. Sprinkle a little **flour** on the surface you're going to knead on. Flour your own hands as well to stop the dough sticking to you. Put the dough on the board or work surface and using the **heel** of your hand (the flat bit attached to your wrist) push down into the dough and away from you. **Fold** the dough over – any way you like – and do it again. Keep doing this until the dough feels like the recipe says it should feel. It takes a bit of time and is quite tiring. If the dough starts **sticking** to your hands or the board, just sprinkle a little more flour over them and the board.

If you have a **food processor** with a dough hook (a white plastic blade) then use that. It takes only a few minutes to knead dough this way and should be done on a moderate to fast speed. Ask for help if you need it.

MAKING BREADCRUMBS . . .

. . . couldn't be simpler. It's best to use bread that's been around for a few days so it's quite dry. Break the bread into chunks and put it into a liquidiser or food processor. Put the lid on and whiz until you've got breadcrumbs. One slice of bread makes a lot of crumbs! If you don't have any old bread, lightly toast your fresh bread, then make it into crumbs. Toasting helps to dry the bread out a bit.

MAKING MORE . . .

. . . is not a problem so long as you've got enough ingredients. If a recipe is for two people and you want to cook for four, just **double** all the quantities. Double them as though you're cooking for **two** or four or **six** or **eight** and so on. It's too difficult judging quantities for three or five or seven people. Stick to your 2 x table!

MARINATING . . .

. . . is when you leave food to **soak** up juices before cooking it. You might use orange juice, lemon juice, soy sauce, oil or herbs to make a marinade. The idea is to leave the food soaking in the marinade for several **hours** – usually the dish is covered and kept in the fridge. Sometimes food can be left for days in its marinade. Not only does this add extra **flavour** but also helps to **soften** meats.

MELTING BUTTER . . .

. . . is Easy Peasy. Put the butter into a small **saucepan** over a low heat on the cooker and wait for it to melt. If the heat is too high it will fizz, bubble, turn brown and burn quite quickly. So watch it. If you're frying eggs you need the butter hot and fizzing but not burning. You can also melt butter in the microwave using a microwave dish. It only takes a few seconds so watch carefully. Ask for help if you need it.

ROLLING OUT . . .

. . . dough or pastry is not the easiest of jobs. If you're using pastry that's been in the freezer, make sure it's completely **defrosted** before you start. Here's how you roll it: use a clean board sprinkled with a little **flour**. Also sprinkle your **rolling pin**. All this sprinkling stops the pastry or dough sticking. If your pastry or dough is in a heap or a ball then begin by pressing the rolling pin down into the middle of it and gently **pushing** away from you. **Turn** the pastry or dough around and roll over it again. Keep doing this until you've got the right shape. It's never perfect but it doesn't matter. You can even use your **fingertips** to press the pastry or dough into the right shape. Try it.

SHREDDING . . .

. . . is just a fancy name for very finely cut **strips** of something. You can shred a lettuce or a cabbage. Think of the phrase 'tearing something to shreds' and you'll get the picture.

SIMMERING . . .

. . . usually happens in a recipe after liquid has boiled. The heat is then turned right down so the liquid just **gently** fizzes and **shimmers** a bit – like it's about to boil but can't get quite hot enough.

SKINNING A PEACH . . .

. . . is a very satisfying thing to do, but peaches need to be **ripe** – quite soft to the touch. Put the peaches into a heatproof bowl and **stab** them a few times with a fork. Boil the kettle and carefully pour **boiling water** over them until they're just covered. Watch out for the hot steam. After a few minutes, lift one out using a slotted spoon or the fork. The skin should be **peeling** off. Just pull the rest off with your fingers. Remember the peaches will be hot and you may have to let them cool a bit before skinning them. You can skin **nectarines** like this as well.

TENDERISING . . .

. . . is another word for **softening** meats. Cooking meat on a very low temperature for a very long time makes it soft and tender. So does leaving it to soak in a **marinade** before you cook it.

TESTING . . .

. . . Is it ready? Yes or no? Making sure a **cake** is properly cooked is very important and very easy. Get a **skewer** or something long, metal and thin. Using your oven gloves, carefully take the cake out of the oven, and **push** the skewer gently into the **middle**. Pull it out and if the tip is all cakey then it needs another 5-10 minutes in the oven. If the tip is clean, then the cake is cooked.

If you're testing **vegetables**, use a skewer or the tip of a sharp knife and push it into the thickest part of the vegetable – the stalk or the biggest potato. If it slides in without you having to push, then it's ready.

Testing **chicken** is very important. Using your oven gloves, carefully take the chicken out of the oven and put it somewhere safe. Stick a skewer or the tip of a sharp knife into a thick bit – a thigh perhaps. If the juice runs out **clear**, it's ready. If the juice is a bit **bloody**, put the chicken straight back into the oven. Cook it for a bit longer and then test it again. Undercooked chicken can be **dangerous**.

TIPPING OUT A CAKE . . .

. . . without dropping it or burning yourself requires bravery – which you've got. Here's how: put a **wire cooling rack** upside down (with its feet in the air) on top of the cake in its tin. Keep your **oven gloves** on. Now carefully wiggle the tin and rack towards the edge of the work surface until there's enough space to slip your gloved hand **underneath** the tin. Keep your other hand firmly on top of the rack. Now you'll have a **sandwich** – hand, wire rack, cake tin and your other hand. Now turn the lot **upside down**. Slide the tin off the cake and leave it to cool. It doesn't matter two hoots if the cake **breaks**. It still tastes gorgeous. It just doesn't look so pretty. The more you do this, the easier it gets.

TOPPING AND TAILING . . .

. . . is another a fancy name for taking a small slice off both ends of a vegetable – from its **top** and its **bottom** or tail.

WHISKING . . .

. . . is quite hard work. You usually whisk eggs or cream. It's a way of **mixing** very fast – often to combine watery liquids, to mix a yolk with its white, to make cream stiff or to remove lumps. You can use an ordinary **fork** for whisking but some people prefer a **whisk**. To see what a hand whisk and an electric whisk look like, turn to pages 22 and 24.

Easy peasy Helpful Tips

CANS . . .

. . . often cause confusion. What's small, medium or large? Use these quantities as a guide. If they don't match perfectly, use your common sense: a **small** can will be around 220g. A **medium** can will be about 400g. A **large** can will be larger than that. Then we have tins. A small tin of tuna can be between 80-100g. You can work out medium and large.

FRESHNESS . . .

. . . can be a **problem** when buying and cooking vegetables. A simple rule is don't buy or cook something if it's yellowing, browning, limp, wrinkled or smelly. If you're not sure then buy some frozen vegetables.

HELP . . .

. . . yourself. If you like cooking, learn to **clear up** after you've finished. That way no one nags you about the mess or bans you from the kitchen until the weekend. The fastest way is to do it as you go along. Fill a sink with **hot, soapy water** so you can drop things in as you finish with them. Instead of using every knife in the kitchen, use just one for meat and one for vegetables. Wash and **dry** them carefully between jobs. Keep the **bin lid** open so you can shovel the rubbish in as you make it. Also, remember to **wipe** down and clean the work surface between each job.

OVEN TEMPERATURES . . .

. . . are difficult. Everyone's oven is different. Make sure your oven has reached the right temperature before you put something into it. If it's an electric oven, it's normally **ready** when the **little red light** goes out. Some ovens cook faster than others, so allow 5-10 minutes more or less cooking time than a recipe says. The more you cook, the better you'll know how your oven works. **Don't** be tempted to **keep opening** the door. You may be thrilled at what you see but every time you open the door the temperature goes down a few degrees and your cooking won't be up to scratch.

STICKY PANS . . .

. . . are **horrible**. Cooking eggs, roasting meat, cooking with milk or frying – all add up to a hot, sticky pan that's difficult to clean. When you've finished cooking, let the pan **cool** down a bit (hot pans don't like being plunged into water) and then leave it to **soak** in hot, soapy water. Sometimes a little dishwasher powder and some hot water will do the trick.

Easy peasy Bits and bobs

ELECTRIC WHISKS . . .

. . . take all the hard work out of whisking cakes, meringues, eggs, mayonnaise – anything that needs it. Turn to page 22 to see what one looks like. You can also use a hand-held rotary whisk, if you've got one.

FOOD PROCESSORS . . .

. . . are great things. They do everything – grate, chop, mix, knead. If you've got one then get help and learn how to use it. Turn to page 23 to see what one looks like.

HAND-HELD ELECTRIC BLENDERS . . .

. . . are brilliant. Turn to page 22 to see what one looks like. The only thing you need to remember is that they can **splash**. So take care if you don't want to cover yourself and the kitchen ceiling.

A HEATPROOF JUG . . .

. . . is a jug that won't crack when you pour boiling liquid into it.

LIQUIDISERS . . .

. . . are convenient – if you've got one in your kitchen. To see what they look like, turn to page 22. To use one, all you do is **pile** all the ingredients in. Take care not to put in too much – you may have to do a bit at a time. Put on the lid, and switch on. Keep **whizzing** until whatever you're making is the right **thickness** or **smoothness**. Sometimes you need to stop the liquidiser and push the ingredients down the jug so they all get mashed up properly.

AN OVENPROOF DISH . . .

. . . means a dish that can go in a hot oven without breaking. Ask an adult if you aren't sure whether a dish is OK to use.

SPOONS . . .

. . . are not always in the right drawer when we need them. If you can't find a measuring spoon that actually says '**tablespoon**' on it, then use a soup spoon. A dessertspoon means a **pudding** spoon and a **teaspoon** means a teaspoon!

Laying the Table the Easy peasy way

Eating together is a very nice thing to do after you've spent the time cooking something delicious. It's not hard. When you lay the table, each person needs:

1. a knife and fork – knife on the right, fork on the left.
2. a drinking glass – sits above the knife.
3. a spoon if you're having pudding – sits next to the knife on its inside. If you've got a pudding that needs cutting, then put a little fork inside the big fork.
4. a side plate if you're having bread – sits next to the fork on its outside.
5. a napkin – sits on the side plate or on the table next to the fork.
6. a soup spoon if you're having soup – sits next to the knife on its outside.
7. table mats if you need them – some for plates and some for serving bowls and dishes.
8. large spoons for serving the food.
9. eating plates.
10. salt and pepper.
11. a jug for water or whatever you drink.
12. a small dish for butter if you're having bread and a little butter knife.
13. a small knife for buttering your bread that you can lay on the napkin.

Each set of cutlery and plates is called a **place setting**.

If you've made supper for **friends** then you could put some candles on the table and maybe a little vase of **flowers** or fresh leaves.

Liquidiser/blender

hand-held electric whisk

hand-held electric blender

metal cooking spoon

Large, medium and small saucepans

Pots & Pans & Things

Weighing Scales

Food processor

Air-tight containers

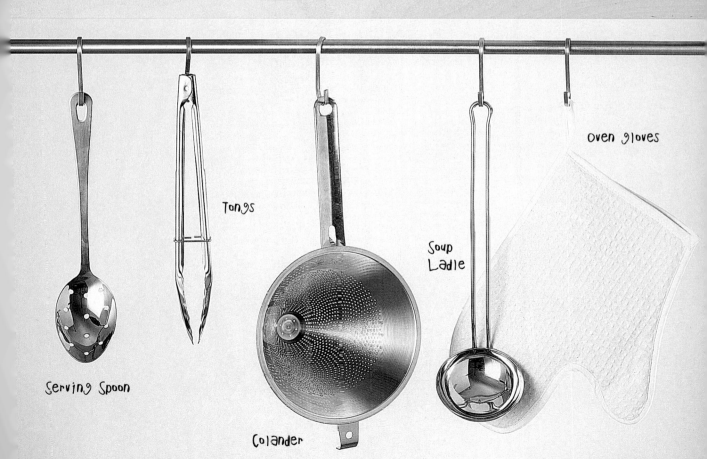

Tongs

oven gloves

Soup
Ladle

Serving Spoon

Colander

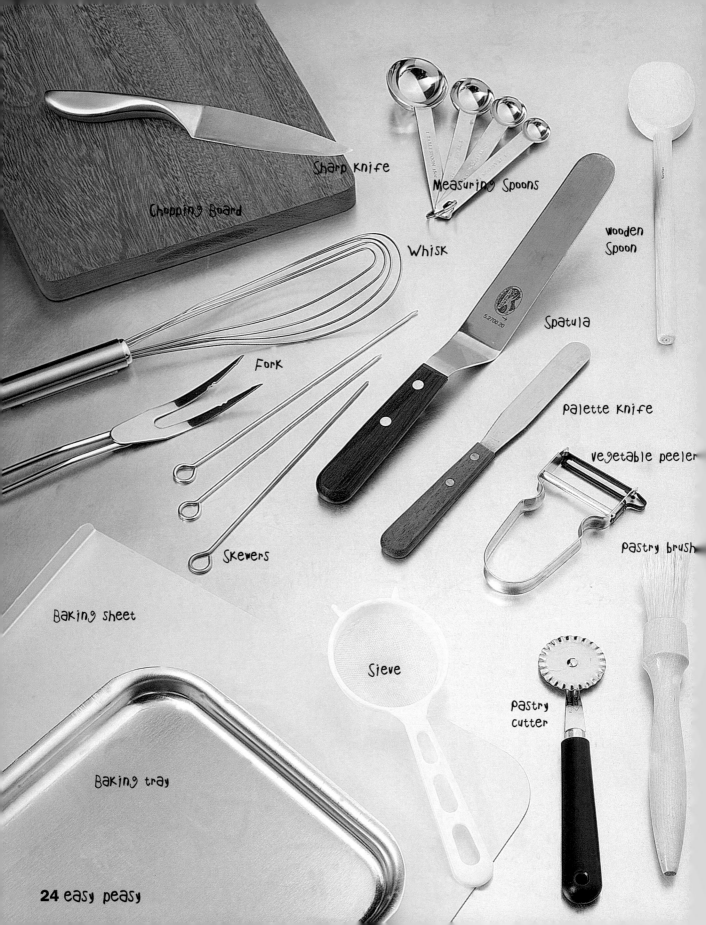

Sharp Knife

Chopping Board

Measuring Spoons

Wooden Spoon

Whisk

Spatula

Fork

palette knife

vegetable peeler

Skewers

pastry brush

Baking sheet

Sieve

pastry cutter

Baking tray

24 easy peasy

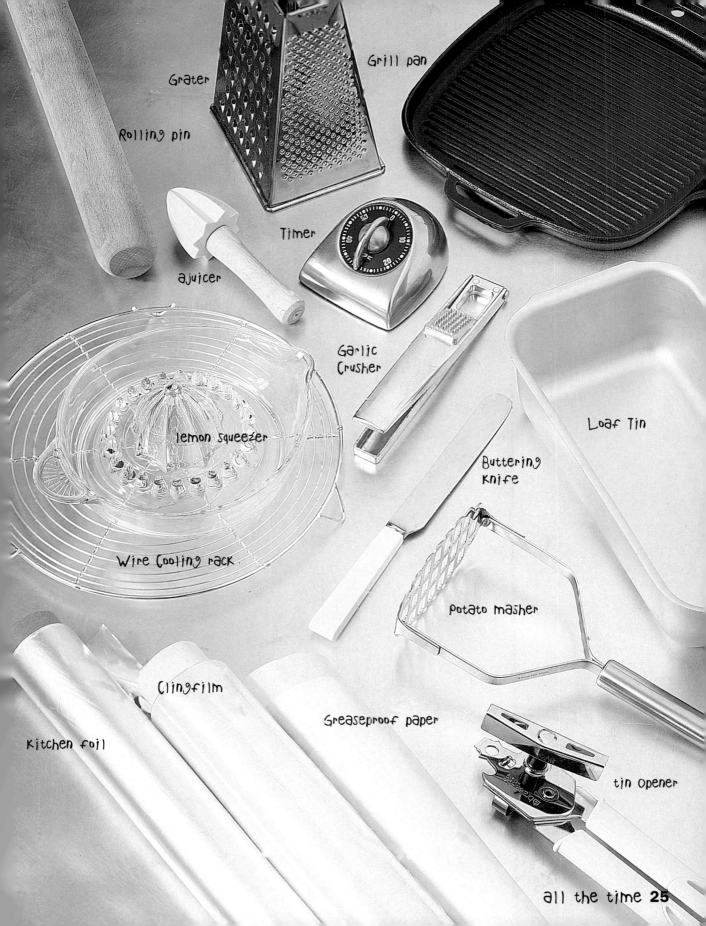

Rolling pin

Grater

Grill pan

ajuicer

Timer

Garlic
Crusher

lemon squeezer

Loaf Tin

Buttering
Knife

Wire Cooling rack

potato masher

Clingfilm

Greaseproof paper

Kitchen foil

tin Opener

Wakey Wakey

Some of us just can't get going in the morning. Our eyes are open but we're still asleep. Breakfast is a brilliant way to wake up our bodies. It's better than a cold shower or a squirt of shaving foam in the face. And it's got to be better than listening to an adult calling and shouting 'Come on! Get up! You're going to be late!'

Breakfast does the job better than anything. But be gentle. Remember you and your body have got to spend the day together. Crisps and coke or sugary cereal will feel like a spurt of life but will actually send your body back to sleep. Your energy won't last long and you'll be knackered by lunch time. If you can't face toast or cereal have some milk and a banana, a piece of cheese or some stewed fruits (see Such a Softy on page 36). You'll be surprised how cheery you'll feel if you manage a good breakfast. Get up a tiny bit earlier and take 10 minutes to make breakfast. Sit down and eat it in 3, maybe 5. Kiss anyone who's around at that time of the morning and skip off to school!

interesting fact

Breakfast is the meal you break your fast with. 'Fast' meaning not eating or drinking for a long period of time – like while you're sleeping.

another interesting fact

Breakfast can be eggs, meat, cheese, breads, sweet rice, pastries, fruits or yoghurts, depending on where in the world you live.

Hold on a minute!

- Remember to be prepared. **Get everything ready** before you start. That means **washing your hands** as well!

- Remember that if you don't understand something or haven't done it before, look back to **Easy Peasy How to do Everything All the Time** on page 10 or **Pots and Pans and Things** on page 22.

- Remember only use **sharp knives**. Blunt ones can be dangerous. Take care when you're using them.

- Remember to use your **oven gloves** when something is hot.

- Remember to **turn off the oven, cooker or grill** when you've finished cooking.

- Remember to **enjoy yourself** and to **ask for help** if you need it.

WAKEY WAKEY

30 **TOMATOES À LA ERIC**

32 **EGG IN A HOLE – JUST FOR YOU**

34 **MONKEY MASH**

35 **A DELICIOUS BREAKFAST**

36 **SUCH A SOFTY**

38 **DEB – DEAD EASY BREAD**

40 **TEA 4 TWO**

42 **EGGIE PIGGIES**

43 **NO FRY – FRY UP**

44 **BOOF BOOF**

46 **BREAD AND CHEESE PLEASE**

Tomatoes à la Eric

You will need 5 ingredients:

4 large, ripe tomatoes
a large blob of butter
some salt and pepper
some sugar
2 slices of bread

some kitchen paper
a chopping board and a sharp knife
a small frying pan
a teaspoon and a wooden spoon
a toaster

1. Wash the tomatoes and dry them with some kitchen paper. Chop them up any way you like.
2. Melt the butter in the frying pan over a medium heat. When it starts to sizzle, put in the tomatoes, a little pinch of salt and pepper and a teaspoon of sugar.
3. Give it all a good stir and let the tomatoes cook for about 10-15 minutes until they've gone all soft, thick and slushy. Stir them occasionally to stop them sticking to the pan.
4. Taste them and add more salt, sugar or pepper if you want. Remember they'll be very hot.
5. Put the bread into the toaster. When it's done, carefully pile the cooked tomatoes onto the toast and eat them while they're still warm.

extra bite
• When I was a child and was ill, all I wanted was comfort food. My mum used to give me Tomatoes à la Mum. Cook the tomatoes in the same way as Tomatoes à la Eric. In a separate bowl, crack 2 eggs and whisk them with a fork. Then tip them into the hot, mushy tomatoes in the frying pan and stir them around until the eggs are cooked – yellowy-red-browny and getting firm.

Watch out
• The trouble with tomatoes is their skins. If you want to get rid of them either pick them out as you go (careful – they'll be hot) or skin them first. Skinning tomatoes is Easy Peasy (see page 13).

Egg in a hole – Just for you

You will need 4 ingredients:

a slice of bread
1 egg
a blob of butter
some salt

a pastry cutter (about 6cm round)
a cup
a frying pan small enough to hold a slice
of bread
a spatula
a plate

1. Cut out a circle of bread from the middle of the slice with the pastry cutter. Keep the circle.
2. Carefully crack the egg into the cup taking care not to break the yolk. Fish out any bits of shell.
3. Heat a blob of butter in the frying pan, on a medium heat, until it starts to fizz.
4. Put the circle of bread into the butter and let it cook for a minute or so until it's brown on its bottom.
5. Using the spatula, carefully lift the bread out of the frying pan and put it on the plate.
6. If all the butter has disappeared add another little blob and when that's fizzing put in the slice of bread that you cut the circle from.
7. Now carefully tip the egg into the hole in the bread and let it cook until it looks ready and how you like it – probably 3-4 minutes. Add a little salt if you want.
8. Put the bread circle on top of the egg and carefully lift the whole thing out of the frying pan with the spatula. Eat it quickly before everyone wants one.

Watch out
• The trouble with cooking eggs like this is the mess they leave in the frying pan. When you've finished cooking put the pan somewhere safe to cool down for a bit. Then let it soak in hot, soapy water before you clean it.

Monkey Mash

You will need 3 ingredients:

2 small (or 1 large) ripe bananas
some milk
a little brown sugar, if you want

a fork and a bowl
a spoon

1. Unzip the banana. Use the fork to mash it in the bowl until it's all soft and gooey.
2. Pour over some milk and a sprinkling of brown sugar – if you must!

extra bites
• Monkey Mash is rather good with a sprinkling of brown sugar and some cinnamon.
• Try mashing a banana onto a piece of warm toast or some buttered, brown bread.

GOOD FOR A SNACK & AFTER SCHOOL

A Delicious Breakfast

You will need 5 ingredients:

150g of pudding rice or short-grain
    round rice
200ml of cold water
1 pint of milk
60g of demerara sugar
some vanilla essence

weighing scales
a measuring jug
a medium saucepan with a lid
a wooden spoon

GOOD FOR A SNACK

1. Weigh out the rice and put it into the saucepan with the water on the cooker. Bring it to the boil on a high heat.

2. When it starts to bubble, lower the heat and put on the lid. Let the rice cook for about 5 minutes until the water has gone. Check it to make sure the rice doesn't dry up and stick to the bottom of the saucepan. You can always add a little more water to stop this happening.

3. Now add the milk, the sugar and a few drops of vanilla essence.

4. Bring it to the boil again. Lower the heat, put on the lid and cook for about 25-30 minutes until the rice is soft. Stir it often to stop it sticking.

5. Taste the rice carefully because it'll be hot. Add more sugar or vanilla essence if you want.

6. Eat this cold for breakfast with Such a Softy (see page 36) or hot for pudding.

extra bites

• A good sprinkling of nutmeg over the top is especially good.

• If you eat this hot, try it with a dessertspoon of raspberry or strawberry jam and a drop of extra milk or cream poured over the top.

• If you want it cold, tip it into a small dish so that it's thickly spread. Let it go cold and then cut into squares and eat it in your fingers. Yes, seriously!

• Instead of sugar try using 4 tablespoons of runny honey.

Such a Softy

You will need 4 ingredients:

3 pears
3 apples
about 100ml of cold water
some sugar, if you want

a chopping board and a sharp knife
a medium saucepan with a lid
a wooden spoon
a potato masher

1. Wash all the fruit under cold, running water. Peel it and take out the pips and cores.

2. Chop up all the fruit any old how and put it into the saucepan with the water.

3. Put on the lid and leave it to cook over a low heat until the fruit is soft and mushy. This will take 15-20 minutes depending on how ripe the fruit is. Stir it occasionally and add some extra water if it starts to get dry.

4. Taste the fruit carefully – it'll be hot – and add some sugar if you want. Leave it to cool and mash it with the masher if you want a purée. You could just leave it soft and chunky. You decide. Eat it cold or warm.

extra bites

• Serve this with A Delicious Breakfast (see page 35).
• Sprinkle some cinnamon over it.
• Serve it on its own or with cream, ice-cream or yoghurt.

• Try cooking it with a handful of sultanas.
• Instead of apples and pears, follow the same recipe using apples and strawberries.
• Instead of water, cook it with apple juice.
• Ripe peaches and raspberries are very good. You don't need to mash this combination. The peaches just need to be sliced into segments before cooking them. Skinning the peaches first is a good idea. See page 16 for how to skin a peach.
• You can use most combinations of fruit for this – plums, nectarines, apricots and cherries. Some will need mashing and some won't. It really depends on what sort of texture you like – smooth or lumpy. If you use cherries, stew them whole but remember they will have stones in them. So don't give them to your baby brother or sister or your granny without warning them first!

Watch out

• The trouble with making Such a Softy is judging how much water or fruit juice to use. If the fruits are hard like apples and pears, then they need about 100ml of water or apple juice to get them going. If you're using soft fruits they probably only need 50ml of liquid because they're juicy fruits to start with. The more you experiment the better judge you will become. Just remember to keep your eye on it and add more liquid if it looks like drying up.

DEB - Dead Easy Bread

You will need 5 ingredients:

225g of self-raising flour
25g of cold butter, cut in pieces
½ tablespoon of golden caster sugar
½ teaspoon of salt
150ml of milk

*a lightly greased baking tray and very
    clean hands*
weighing scales
a sieve and a large bowl
a tablespoon and a teaspoon
a measuring jug for the milk
a wooden spoon
a sharp knife and a pastry brush
oven gloves
a timer

1. Turn on the oven to 200°C/400°F/
gas mark 6.
2. Grease the baking tray with a little butter.
Use your fingers or some kitchen paper.
3. Sieve the flour into the bowl and using
your (clean, please!) fingers, rub in the
butter until there are no lumps left and
the mixture looks like breadcrumbs.
4. Add the sugar and salt and mix it well.
5. Now pour the milk into the middle of the
flour and mix it together with the wooden
spoon until you have a soft dough.
6. Put some flour on your hands – to stop
the dough sticking to you – and mould the
dough into a ball. You may need to flour
your hands a few times and you'll have
to do a bit of pinching and pushing.
7. Put the ball of dough onto the baking tray
and flatten it a bit with the heel of your
hand. That's the bit where your hand joins
your wrist! It should look like a fat frisbee.
8. Using your sharp knife, slice the dough
into four quarters but be careful not to cut
all the way through. Just about half way.
9. With the pastry brush, brush some milk
over the top and using your oven gloves,
put the tray into the oven. Set the timer
for about 20-25 minutes.

10. When the time is up, check whether the bread is cooked by looking at the bits where you cut with the knife. They should look dry and crumbly and the whole loaf should be nicely brown. If it doesn't look like this, cook it for another 5 minutes. Eat it straight away or very soon after you've cooked it. It only stays fresh for about a day.

extra bites
• There are millions of things you can do with DEB. Try adding a handful of mixed, dried fruit to the flour before you pour in the milk.
• Add a couple of handfuls of grated cheese to the flour before you pour in the milk. You could even sprinkle some on top before it goes into the oven.
• Best of all is to eat it hot with butter and jam.

GOOD FOR A SNACK
GOOD FOR LUNCHBOXES

Watch out
• The trouble with DEB is that she's irresistible. Try not to eat the whole thing before you even get it to the table. If one loaf is not enough, make two!

Tea 4 Two

You will need 4 ingredients:

some water
2 tea bags
some milk
sugar, if you want

a kettle
2 mugs
a teaspoon
a little patience

1. Fill the kettle with fresh, cold water and switch it on. You may want some adult help for this.
2. Put a tea bag in each mug and as soon as the kettle has boiled, carefully pour the boiling water over the tea bags. Remember to leave room for the milk.
3. Leave the tea to brew for about 2 minutes.
4. Then carefully take out the tea bags with the teaspoon – giving each one a little squeeze on the inside of the mug.
5. Stir in as much milk as you need – until it's the right colour for you. Add some sugar if you want.
6. Now go and watch some telly.

extra bites
• Try experimenting with different kinds of tea. Instead of adding milk, just let the tea brew for a minute and then add a slice of lemon and some sugar. Tea without milk is called black tea.
• You could even let it go cold and then throw in a handful of ice cubes to make iced tea.
• Black tea is nicest with a weaker kind of tea. Try using Earl Grey or fruit teas. They're all made without milk and they can be very refreshing. Remember *The Story of Peter Rabbit?* His mother gave him soothing camomile tea before he went to bed.

Watch out
• The trouble with tea is working out how you like it. The longer you leave it to brew the stronger it will be. You need also to experiment with how much milk you like. The more you make tea, the easier and better it gets.

Eggie Piggies

**For each person you will need
5 ingredients:**

2 eggs
2 tablespoons of milk
salt and pepper
some thin strips of ham
a blob of butter

a small bowl and a fork or whisk
a tablespoon
a frying pan
a wooden spoon
a big appetite

1. Break the eggs into the bowl.
Remember to fish out any bits of shell.
2. Add the milk and a little salt and pepper.
Whisk them thoroughly and add the ham.
3. Melt the butter in the frying pan over a
medium heat. When it starts to sizzle, add
the egg mixture.
4. Keep stirring it around with the wooden
spoon so it doesn't stick to the frying pan.
When it looks cooked enough for you –
about 3 minutes – eat at once. Nice with
toast and tea or a glass of milk.

Watch out

• Eggs go on cooking for a while after you've
taken them off the heat. So it's best to eat
them straight away before they turn into
yellow rocks.
• The trouble with cooking eggs like this
is the mess they leave in the frying pan.
When you've finished cooking, put the pan
somewhere safe to cool down for a bit.
Then let it soak in some hot, soapy water
before you clean it.

No Fry – Fry up

You will need 6 ingredients:

500g of sausages
some soft butter
4 or 5 tomatoes
250g of mushrooms
4 eggs
some salt and pepper

*an ovenproof dish, big enough to hold
   the sausages*
oven gloves
kitchen tongs
some kitchen paper
a chopping board and a sharp knife
a small bowl for the eggs and a fork

1. Turn on the oven to 200°C/400°F/
gas mark 6.
2. Put the sausages into the ovenproof
dish and use your oven gloves to
carefully put them into the oven.
3. After 15 minutes, put on your oven
gloves and take the dish out of the oven.
Put it somewhere safe and turn the
sausages over with kitchen tongs. Then
put them back for another 15 minutes.

4. When the sausages are well cooked
and brown all over, carefully take them out
of the oven (remember to use your oven
gloves) and drain them on some kitchen
paper. If there's a lot of fat in the dish get
rid of most of it by carefully soaking it up
with kitchen paper. Take care not to burn
yourself!
5. Now carefully slice the sausages with a
sharp knife and put them back into the dish.
6. Wash, dry and chop the tomatoes and
mushrooms any old how. Add them to the
sausages and mix it all thoroughly.
7. Crack the eggs into the little bowl – fish
out any bits of shell – and whisk them. Pour
them over the sausages and add some salt
and pepper.
8. Using your oven gloves, put the whole
lot back in the oven for 20-30 minutes
until the egg is set and the tomatoes
look mushy.

extra bites
- Very good with toast.
- Very filling.
- You can always leave out the mushrooms!

VERY GOOD FOR A WEEKEND BREAKFAST

Boof Boof

This is for anyone who doesn't know what to have for breakfast.

You will need 9 ingredients:

some slices of ham
some hard-boiled eggs – 1 for each
   person (see page 14)
some slices of cheese
some sweet bread – hot cross buns
   or croissants
some crusty white bread or rolls
some butter and some jam
some natural yoghurt
some fresh fruit – peeled and sliced –
   or some stewed fruit (see Such
   a Softy on page 36)
a jug of cold milk or fresh fruit juice

serving bowls and plates for the food
each person will need a plate, a bowl,
   a knife, a spoon and a glass (see
   Laying the Table the Easy Peasy Way
   on page 21)
some napkins (paper or cloth)
plenty of time

1. Put all the food into serving bowls and plates.
2. Pour the yoghurt into a bowl and put a spoon in it.
3. Do the same with the jam.
4. Put the butter onto a small dish and give it a little knife.
5. Peel and slice the fruits you're using and arrange them on a large, flat plate or in a large bowl. If you're serving Such a Softy, then put the stewed fruit into a serving bowl with a spoon.
6. Now lay the table. Put all the food and drink on the table or on the side. Lay a place for each person with a plate, a bowl, a knife, a spoon, a glass and a napkin.
7. Wake up the rest of the household and tell them breakfast is ready!

extra bites

• You need time and energy to prepare this breakfast. It's great to do at weekends or when you've had a sleep-over.
• You could even have a birthday breakfast instead of a birthday tea.

Bread and Cheese please

You will need 5 ingredients:

2 slices of bread – any bread
some butter
some grated Cheddar cheese
some Worcestershire sauce
some black pepper

a grill and a grill pan
a chopping board
a spreading knife
oven gloves

1. Turn on the grill. (Ask for help if you need it.) Toast one side of the bread.
2. Spread a thin layer of butter over the uncooked side and pile on the grated cheese.
3. Sprinkle a few drops of Worcestershire sauce and a little black pepper over the top.
4. Using your oven gloves, carefully put it under the grill and let the cheese cook until it starts to go brown and gets a bit bubbly.

extra bites

• You can also add some thinly sliced tomatoes and a little salt. This gives it another flavour and makes it a bit juicier.
• If you're feeling a bit wild, mix some thin strips of ham into the cheese before piling it onto the toast.
• If you like it a bit crunchier, then toast the bread on both sides first.

Watch out

• Cooked cheese gets very hot. So be careful you don't burn your tongue.
• The trouble with grilling is the grill pan always gets so dirty. You can save yourself a lot of washing up by lining the grill pan with some kitchen foil before cooking on it. That way you can just crumple up the foil and throw it away at the end.

GOOD FOR A SNACK

Any Time

Do you ever eat in bed?

a) Always
b) Certainly not
c) Only if I can get away with it

The thought of eating in bed is often better than actually doing it. But you've got to try it to find out. Always make sure the duvet is tucked tightly under your chin so any crumbs stay on top of the bed and don't get stuck in your pyjamas.

The thing about eating in bed is it makes you wonder what foods should be eaten at what times. Why should meatballs only be eaten for lunch or supper? Why not have them for a snack while watching telly? The same goes for other foods. Soups are just as good for lunch as they are ladled into a mug for drinking while you do your homework.

Now, if you were an angel you'd only ever eat breakfast, lunch and supper with not a mouthful in between. But let's get real. We often want something to eat at different times of the day. I've even been known to make toast in the middle of the night. So Any Time shows how all sorts of foods can be eaten at all sorts of times. But try to avoid meringues for breakfast!

interesting fact

In some parts of Germany they eat a second breakfast called zweites Frühstück.

another interesting fact

In my house we often eat a second breakfast too. It's called Jolly Big Snack.

Hold on a minute!

- Remember to be prepared. **Get everything ready** before you start. That means **washing your hands** as well!

- Remember that if you don't understand something or haven't done it before, look back to **Easy Peasy How to do Everything All the Time** on page 10 or **Pots and Pans and Things** on page 22.

- Remember only use **sharp knives**. Blunt ones can be dangerous. Take care when you're using them.

- Remember to use your **oven gloves** when something is hot.

- Remember to **turn off the oven, cooker or grill** when you've finished cooking.

- Remember to **enjoy yourself** and to **ask for help** if you need it.

Any Time

52   **ROLL UPS**

53   **CHOPPED SANDWICH**

54   **STICK-TO-IT**

56   **IT COULD BE LETTUCE**

57   **BOILED**

58   **WELL DRESSED AND COOL**

60   **UNDERGROUND**

61   **FTP!**

62   **BALLS FIRST**

64   **FOWL MEAT LOAF**

66   **IT'S A STICK UP**

68   **PEAPOT**

69   **A SWEET ROAST**

70   **LITTLE WHITE GRAINS – NOT RICE, JUST NICE**

72   **GREEN WITH PEAS**

74   **THICK & STICKY**

75   **IN YOUR FINGERS**

76   **I WANT IT NOW!**

78   **POCKETS**

80   **WHAT'S IN YOUR POCKET?**

81   **STRIPS NOT CHIPS**

82   **EIGHT FOR ME – NONE FOR YOU**

84   **CRACKING GOOD CORN**

85   **CLAPPLE**

86   **YUM – EGG WHITES!**

Roll Ups

You will need 4 ingredients:

2 slices of bread
some soft butter
some Marmite
some cheese

a chopping board and a sharp knife
a knife for butter and Marmite
some clingfilm or kitchen foil

1. Using the sharp knife, carefully cut the crusts off the bread and spread each slice with a thin layer of butter and Marmite.
2. Now cut two long strips of cheese and put them on the edge of each slice of bread. Roll them up and wrap them in clingfilm or kitchen foil until you want to eat them. Make as many Roll Ups as you think you'll be able to eat.

extra bites
• Edam cheese is good for Roll Ups because it's Easy Peasy to cut into strips. Cheese slices are pretty good as well.
• You can use any combination of filling provided it can be rolled up without squidging out of the ends.
• Try a sausage with some tomato ketchup.
• Try soft cheese like Philadelphia which also just happens to be delicious spread with Marmite.
• Try an Edam and marmalade mix. Cheese and marmalade are gorgeous together.

GOOD FOR LUNCH BOXES
GOOD FOR BED

Chopped Sandwich

**For 1 sandwich you will need
6 ingredients:**

1 egg
2-3 small cherry tomatoes
half a spring onion
some salt and pepper
some butter
2 slices of bread

*a small saucepan
a timer or a clock
some kitchen paper
a chopping board and a sharp knife
a small bowl
a small pastry cutter
a knife for buttering*

1. Put the egg in the saucepan with enough cold water to cover it. Bring it to the boil over a high heat and cook it for 7-8 minutes, depending on how big it is (see hard-boiling eggs on page 14). To check if the egg is ready, carefully lift it out of the saucepan. If the water disappears quite quickly and leaves the shell looking dry, you'll know it's cooked.
2. Put the saucepan in the sink and run cold water from the tap over it to cool it down and stop it cooking. Leave it in the water while you prepare the rest.
3. Wash and dry the tomatoes and spring onion. Cut the tomatoes into very small chunks and the spring onion into tiny bits. Put them into the bowl.

4. Peel the hard-boiled egg by tapping the shell all over on the work surface until it cracks and crumples. Roll it between your hands and the shell should come off quite easily.
5. Put the egg into the bowl and chop it all up using the pastry cutter until it looks like mush. Add a little salt and pepper and sandwich the lot between two buttered slices of bread.

extra bites
• If you don't like spring onions, leave it out.
• Try adding a dessertspoon of mayonnaise to make the filling richer.
• Try adding some bacon. Put a small, non-stick frying pan on the cooker and let it warm up over a medium heat for a couple of minutes. Put in a slice of streaky bacon and cook it until it's crisp. If the bacon is very dry, you could add a drop of vegetable oil to the frying pan. When it's ready drain the bacon on some kitchen paper and chop it up with everything else.

GOOD FOR LUNCH BOXES

Stick-to-it

You will need 5 ingredients:

1 apple
1 hard pear
a few fresh apricots, if they're in season
some runny honey
a little soft butter

some kitchen paper
a chopping board and a sharp knife
some wooden kebab sticks
a small saucepan or a microwave bowl
a spoon for the honey
a baking tray and a grill
a pastry brush, if you want
oven gloves

1. Turn on the grill. (Ask for help if you need it.)
2. Wash the apricots under cold, running water. Dry them with some kitchen paper and cut them in half. Take out the stones.
3. Peel the apple and pear and take out the core and pips. Chop them into bite-sized chunks.

4. Thread the pieces of fruit onto the kebab sticks leaving enough stick so you can hold them easily. Remember to mix and match the colours. Put the fruit kebabs onto the baking tray.
5. Put a blob of butter and a big dollop of runny honey into the saucepan and warm over a low heat until the butter melts. Stir it carefully. If you're using the microwave to do this, remember to use a microwave bowl.
6. Now pour the honey mixture all over the kebabs making sure they're well coated. You could use a pastry brush to mop up the last bits if you want to.
7. Using your oven gloves, pop the kebabs under the grill and leave them until they start to go brown around the edges. When this happens, put on your oven gloves and carefully pull out the baking tray. Turn the kebabs over and grill the other side.
8. If you want to eat these hot, it's best to slide the pieces off the kebab sticks and eat them with cocktail sticks. They will be very hot. Otherwise eat them cold straight off the sticks.

extra bites

• You could always use fresh pineapple as well.
• Try serving these with a little dipping bowl of yoghurt or cream.

GOOD FOR FRIENDS

It could be Lettuce

You can use any combination of salad leaves. If you're not using ready-prepared bags from the supermarket then remember to wash everything well and dry it in a salad spinner or in some kitchen paper. Salad leaves like to be torn by hand, not sliced with knives. Metal makes them go brown.

You will need 6 ingredients:

lots of different salad leaves – anything you like
a large handful of chopped, fresh parsley
3 tablespoons of olive oil
1 dessertspoon of lemon juice
1 small clove of chopped garlic
a little pinch of salt, pepper and sugar

a salad bowl
some kitchen paper
a chopping board and a sharp knife
a jar with a lid for the dressing
a tablespoon

1. Put the salad leaves into the bowl. Then wash the parsley under cold, running water and dry it in some kitchen paper. Chop up the parsley as small as you can and put it in the bowl.

2. Now make the dressing by putting all the rest of the ingredients into the jar and shaking it. Take the lid off the jar and smell. Taste the dressing and add more of any of the ingredients you need. (If it's too sharp, add a little more sugar. If it's too oily add a bit more lemon juice.)

3. Pour the dressing over the salad and mix it well. If you want more dressing just double the quantities.

extra bites

• You can add endless salady things to a plain, green salad. Try some finely chopped spring onions and other chopped, fresh herbs like coriander or basil. In fact, anything you fancy as long as it's green.

• If you want to turn your salad into a meal, sprinkle some grated cheese into it or chop up 2 hard-boiled eggs (see page 14) and even add some flaked tuna.

• If you want to be a salad dressing star, try adding a tablespoon of grated Parmesan cheese to your dressing.

• If you don't want to use all the dressing, you can keep it for a few days in the fridge.

Boiled

You will need 3 ingredients:

some little, new potatoes – as many
  as you think everyone will eat
some cold water
some salt

*a vegetable scrubbing brush (if you've
  got one)*
*a saucepan with a lid – big enough
  to hold all the potatoes*
a fork
oven gloves
a colander, placed in the sink
a serving dish

1. Scrub the potatoes in cold, running water making sure you scrape off any mud or grit.
2. Put them in the saucepan with enough cold water to cover them.
3. Sprinkle in some salt and taste the water. It should be salty.
4. Put the lid on the saucepan. Put it on the cooker and turn the heat up high. When the water is bubbling crossly – that's boiling – turn the heat down and leave the potatoes to cook slowly in gently bubbling water – that's simmering.

5. The potatoes should be cooked after about 10-15 minutes, depending on how big or small they are. Test them by pushing the fork into a couple of them. (Be careful of the hot steam when you take off the lid. It's best to use your oven gloves for this.) If it slides in easily, they're cooked. If not, then cook them a little bit longer and test again.
6. When the potatoes are done, use your oven gloves to carefully take the saucepan to the sink and pour the potatoes into the colander. Remember the saucepan will be heavy, hot and steamy.
7. When all the water has drained away, tip the potatoes out of the colander into the serving dish. Eat them straight away.

extra bites

• For extra gorgeousness add a good-sized blob of butter over the steaming hot potatoes.
• You can also add some chopped, fresh chives or parsley with the butter.
• If you want to charm the pants off somebody, serve these potatoes warm in a special dressing (see Well Dressed and Cool on page 58).

Well Dressed and Cool

You will need 8 ingredients:

hot, boiled potatoes (see page 57)
1 clove of crushed or chopped garlic
6 tablespoons of olive oil
1 tablespoon of white wine vinegar
1 teaspoon of Dijon mustard
some salt
a pinch of sugar
a good handful of chopped, fresh chives
   or parsley

*a garlic crusher or a small chopping
   board and a sharp knife*
a jar with a lid for the dressing
2 tablespoons and a teaspoon
2 large spoons for mixing the potatoes
a serving bowl

1. Peel and chop the garlic into tiny bits.
If you have a crusher there's no need to
peel it – just crush it. Put the chopped
or crushed garlic in the jar.
2. Put all the rest of the dressing
ingredients – except the herbs – into
the jar. Put the lid on and shake the jar
vigorously. Now smell and taste the
dressing. Experiment until you get the
taste you like by adding a little more of
any of the ingredients. Always shake the
dressing well before tasting it.

3. Pour the dressing over the potatoes
while they're still warm. You may not need
all the dressing. Mix them carefully so you
don't break them up too much and then
sprinkle the chopped, fresh herbs over
them. Taste the dressed potatoes and add
more dressing if you need it.
4. You can eat the potatoes straight away
or leave them to go cold. If you eat them
cold, you'll need to mix them again as the
dressing often sinks to the bottom of the
bowl. You may also want to add a little more
dressing. Taste and see.

extra bite

• Try mixing together 4 or 5 tablespoons of
mayonnaise with a squeeze of lemon juice,
a teaspoon of white wine vinegar, a little
garlic and a teeny bit of salt and pepper.
Mix it all together. Shake, smell and taste,
and then pour it over the potatoes.
• If you're making the dressing, watch out
for lemon pips as they always get into
places they shouldn't. Either squeeze the
lemon and then pour the juice through a
small sieve or simply fish out the pips with a
teaspoon. You choose.

GREAT FOR A SNACK

underground

You will need 6 ingredients:

3 baking potatoes
3 carrots
3 leeks
a large blob of butter
some salt and pepper
cold water

a chopping board
a sharp knife and a vegetable peeler
a colander in the sink
a wooden spoon
a large saucepan with a lid
a hand-held electric blender or liquidiser

1. Peel the potatoes and carrots. Prepare the leeks (see page 11).
2. Wash all the vegetables in the colander under cold, running water and cut them into chunks any old how.
3. Melt a large blob of butter in the saucepan over a medium heat.
4. Add all the vegetables and some salt and pepper. Turn them over in the butter using the wooden spoon to make sure they're well covered.
5. Pour in enough cold water to cover the vegetables. Turn the heat up high and wait until the water starts boiling.
6. Now put the lid on and turn the heat down very low. Leave the soup to simmer for about 20-30 minutes depending on how large the chunks are. To test whether the vegetables are cooked, poke the tip of the sharp knife into one of the larger chunks of potato. If it slides in easily, the soup is ready. If it doesn't, cook it for a bit longer.
7. Turn off the heat and let the soup cool for a while. Then whiz it with the hand-held electric blender – take care not to splash the ceiling! Or you can pour the soup, very carefully, into the liquidiser. Put the lid on and whiz until it's right for you. Ask for help with this bit if you need it. Underground is better when it's very smooth.
8. When you're ready to eat the soup, taste it and add more salt if you want or more water if it's too thick. Then warm it up on the cooker over a medium heat. It's especially gorgeous with a blob of cream stirred in just before serving.

FTP!

You will need 5 ingredients:

1 medium (500g) tin of tuna
125g of cream cheese
the juice of half a small lemon
a blob of soft butter
some salt and pepper

a tin opener and a little sieve in the sink
a food processor or a fork and strong
  wrists
a small bowl
a lemon squeezer and a sharp knife

1. Open the tin of tuna and drain it over the sink in the sieve. Tip it into the food processor or the small bowl.

2. Now add the rest of the ingredients and whiz in the food processor or mash well with the fork in the small bowl, until the mixture looks soft enough to spread. Taste it and add more lemon, salt or butter if you want.

extra bites

• Instead of butter you could try 1 table-spoon of mayonnaise. You may need a bit more than 1 tablespoon. Taste it and see.
• FTP is delicious in sandwiches especially with a few chopped spring onions and some very thin slices of cucumber.
• You can make it with tinned sardines instead of tuna.
• It's pretty good with bread sticks (see pages 66-67)
• It's gorgeous on hot, buttered toast.
• And it's great straight off a teaspoon.
• You can even keep it for a few days in an airtight container in the fridge.

GOOD FOR LUNCH BOXES

Balls First

You will need 8 ingredients:

500g of minced lamb, chicken or beef
1 onion
2 cloves of garlic
1 large egg (if you can't eat eggs, then use 2 large handfuls of breadcrumbs instead – see Making Breadcrumbs on page 15)
1-2 tablespoons of Worcestershire sauce
some salt and pepper
some plain flour
4 or 5 tablespoons of vegetable oil for frying

a bowl for mixing all the ingredients
a chopping board and a sharp knife
a tablespoon
a fork or a very clean pair of hands
a small bowl for the flour
a large frying pan
a pair of tongs and some kitchen paper

1. Put the meat into the bowl.
2. Peel the onion and garlic and chop them into tiny, tiny pieces and put them into the bowl. If you've got a food processor, then do it in that (ask for help if you need it).
3. Crack the egg into the bowl – fish out any bits of shell – and add that to the meat with the Worcestershire sauce and some salt and pepper.
4. Mix everything together very well with the fork – or your clean hands. (Remember to wash them thoroughly before and afterwards. Hands are best for proper mixing and squeezing.)
5. Pour some flour into the small bowl. Take a little handful of the mixture and roll it around in the palms of your hands until you've got a little ball. Dip it in and out of the flour. Give it a little shake and put it on the chopping board. Make all the balls like this but keep one crumb!
6. Now, heat the vegetable oil in the frying pan on a medium heat. Add the crumb and when it starts to sizzle, carefully add some balls. Remember hot oil can splash.
7. After a few minutes roll the balls over with the fork so they cook evenly.
8. When they're nice and brown all over, probably after about 12-15 minutes depending on how big they are, carefully lift the balls out of the frying pan with the tongs and let them drain on the kitchen paper. Cook all the balls like this.

extra bites

• Balls First are extra good to eat on their own or while you're washing up or watching telly, especially if you've got a little bowl of tomato ketchup to dunk them into.
• Try cooking Balls – With One Sauce (see page 97).

Fowl Meat Loaf

You will need 8 ingredients:

1 onion
2 cloves of garlic
500g of minced chicken
75g of breadcrumbs (see page 15)
1 egg
some salt and pepper
some Worcestershire sauce
some soft butter

a chopping board and a sharp knife
a large mixing bowl and a wooden
  spoon
some kitchen paper
a non-stick loaf tin
oven gloves

1. Turn on the oven to 180°C/350°F/ gas mark 4.
2. Peel and chop the onion and garlic as small as you can and put into the bowl.
3. Add the chicken, the breadcrumbs, the egg – remember to fish out any bits of shell – some salt and pepper and a few shakings of Worcestershire sauce. (If you have a food processor, you can put everything, except the chicken, into it and just whiz like crazy for a minute or so, until the mixture is all soft and tiny. Then add it to the chicken.)
4. Now wash your hands and start mixing. Lots of mixing is needed. If you can't bear the thought of using your hands, then use the wooden spoon.

5. Wash your hands again. Grease the loaf tin with a little butter – you can use your hands or some kitchen paper. Pile the mixture into the tin and using your oven gloves, carefully put it into the oven for between 45 minutes to 1 hour. You may want to put a bit of greaseproof paper over the top of the loaf for the first 30 minutes. Then take it off and let the top get brown.
6. When it is cooked, let the meat loaf go cold in the tin and then tip it out. Sometimes there's a little puddle of cooking juices on the top and around the sides. Just mop them up with some kitchen paper.

NOT GOOD FOR BED

extra bites
• You can do lots of things with Fowl Meat Loaf. Wrap it up well and look at it for a few days in the fridge or put it in the freezer and forget you ever made it.
• Cut thin slices, add some pickle or ketchup and make sandwiches with it.
• Eat it with salad and little boiled potatoes (see pages 56 and 57).
• Cut it up into little squares, stab cocktail sticks into them and dunk them into some tomato ketchup while you watch telly.
• If you're not keen on chicken, you can make this with minced turkey or beef.
• It's really delicious served with several blobs of One Sauce (see page 96).
• Try also adding a handful of chopped, fresh parsley to the mixture before you cook it.

It's a Stick Up

You will need 6 ingredients:

150ml of warm water from the kettle
1 sachet of instant dried yeast
375g of strong bread flour and a little
  extra for your hands
1 teaspoon of salt
2 tablespoons of olive oil and a little
  extra
1 egg white

a measuring jug
2 teaspoons and a tablespoon
weighing scales and a large bowl
a wooden spoon and some clingfilm
a baking tray
a small bowl and a fork for the egg white
a pastry brush
oven gloves
kitchen tongs and a wire cooling rack

1. Turn on the oven to 220°C/425°F/
gas mark 7.
2. Pour the water into the measuring jug
and stir in the yeast. Leave it until it gets
frothy.
3. Put the flour and salt into the bowl and
pour in the yeast and olive oil. Mix it all
together very well with the wooden spoon.
As it thickens it'll make a ball that will leave
the sides of the bowl.
4. Now put some flour on your hands and
start pushing and folding the dough. This is
called kneading (see page 15). Do this
until it starts to feel quite smooth. Add
more flour to your hands if the dough sticks
to them. If it's dry and crumbly, add a little
more water. You might find it easier to do
this bit on a work surface. But remember
to make sure it's clean before you start.
(If you have a food processor with a dough
hook – a white plastic blade – you can use
it instead for steps 3 and 4.)
5. Put the dough back in the bowl. Tip a
little olive oil into your hand and smooth it
over the top. Cover the bowl with clingfilm,
set the timer and leave it for 30 minutes.
6. When the time is up, the dough will have
risen a little. This is called proving. Take
off the clingfilm and give it a few punches
until it goes flat again. Then knead it for
a minute.
7. Grease your baking tray with a little oil.
Use your fingers (clean hands, please!).
It's much easier.

8. Sprinkle a little flour onto the clean work surface and pull off a small chunk of dough. Roll it into a long, very thin sausage and put it on the baking tray. Sometimes a bit of oil on your hands makes the rolling easier. You'll get the hang of it after the first few. Just think of rolling soft stuff like modelling clay.

9. Roll all the dough like this and then leave the sticks for another 10 minutes.

10. While you're waiting, separate the egg (see page 10) and whisk the white with the fork.

11. Brush each stick with the egg white and using your oven gloves, carefully put them into the oven for 15 minutes. When the time is up, the breadsticks will be quite crisp. Take them carefully out of the oven, using your oven gloves. Put them on the wire cooling rack with the kitchen tongs to let them cool.

These don't last very long so try to eat them the same day. Invite your friends around!

GOOD FOR LUNCH BOXES

extra bites
• If you want to add an extra flavour, mix a tablespoon of sesame seeds into the whisked egg white.
• If you use wholemeal flour, the sticks will have a rougher, more earthy flavour.
• Eat them with everything – soup, butter, honey, cheese.

Watch out
• If you eat breadsticks in bed, be prepared for crumbs!

peapot

You will need 7 ingredients:

1 small onion
1 large clove of garlic
a large blob of butter
2 baking potatoes
some salt
1½ pints of cold water
500g of frozen peas

a chopping board and a sharp knife
a medium saucepan with a lid
a wooden spoon and a measuring jug
oven gloves
weighing scales
a liquidiser or a hand-held electric
  blender

1. Carefully peel and chop the onion and garlic any old how.
2. Put the saucepan on the cooker over a low heat. Add the butter and when it's melted, add the chopped onion and garlic. Cook them slowly for about 5 minutes, stirring from time to time with the wooden spoon.

3. While the onion and garlic are cooking, scrub the potatoes thoroughly under cold, running water. You're not going to peel them so make sure you get rid of all the mud. Chop the potatoes up into medium chunks and add them to the saucepan.
4. Give it all a good stir so the potatoes get covered in the buttery onions. Add a good pinch of salt and the water.
5. Turn up the heat until the soup starts to boil and then lower it right down. Put the lid on and leave it for 15-20 minutes depending on how big your chunks are. To test whether the potatoes are cooked, push the tip of your sharp knife into one of them. (Be careful of the hot steam when you take off the lid. It's best to use your oven gloves for this.) If the knife slides in easily, then the potatoes are ready. If not, then cook them for a bit longer and test again.
6. Add the peas and give the soup a good stir. Turn the heat up to medium, put the lid back on and leave it for another 10 minutes. Taste the soup (take care because it'll be hot) and add more salt if you want.
7. Take the soup off the heat and let it cool for a bit. Then carefully pour it into the liquidiser or use the hand-held electric blender. (Ask for help if you need it.) Put the lid on and whiz until it looks like you want it to look – smooth or lumpy. If it's too thick, just add a little more water.
8. This is very good with It's a Stick Up (see page 66-67).

A Sweet Roast

You will need 8 ingredients:

3 carrots
1 parsnip
1 baking potato
some baby corn
2 cloves of garlic
2 tablespoons of olive oil
some salt
a few sprigs of fresh rosemary or thyme

a vegetable peeler
a chopping board and a sharp knife
some kitchen paper
a large bowl
a tablespoon and a wooden spoon
a large baking tray
oven gloves

1. Turn on the oven to 220°C/425°F/ gas mark 7.
2. Peel the carrots, the parsnip and the potato. Take a thin slice off the tops and bottoms of the parsnip and the carrots. This is called topping and tailing (see page 17).
3. Wash the vegetables under cold, running water. Dry them thoroughly with the kitchen paper and chop them into cubes. Put them into the bowl.

4. Wash and dry the corn and cut them in half if they're very long. If not, just leave them whole. Add them to the bowl.
5. Peel and chop the garlic and put it into the bowl as well.
6. Add the oil, a good sprinkling of salt and the herbs. Mix them together thoroughly.
7. Tip them onto the baking tray and using your oven gloves, carefully put it into the oven for about 40 minutes. The vegetables should be brown round the edges and slightly shrivelled up.

extra bites
• Roasted vegetables are nearly as delicious when they're cold.
• You can try other kinds of vegetables – peppers and courgettes, baby onions and aubergines. These are specially good if you mix them through some warm cous cous (see page 70).
• You can use other herbs like fresh basil.
• Try dipping the vegetables into salad cream or mayonnaise.

GOOD FOR FRIENDS AND SNACKS

Little White Grains –

Private Message:

Cous cous sounds boring. But wait. You'll be amazed what you can do with it – sweet or savoury. First you need to know how to make it. Then you need to know how to turn it into something really gorgeous. Here goes . . .

You will need 4 ingredients:

150g of instant cous cous
a teaspoon of salt
250ml of boiling water from the kettle
2 tablespoons of vegetable or
   groundnut oil

*weighing scales
a large bowl and a fork
a teaspoon and a tablespoon
a heatproof measuring jug
some clingfilm*

1. Put the cous cous and the salt into the bowl. Mix the salt in with the fork.
2. Pour the boiling water into the cous cous and fork it around a bit to break up the grains.
3. Cover it with clingfilm and leave it for about 10 minutes until all the water has gone and the grains are nice and soft.
4. Before you serve it, add the oil and fork it around again to break up the grains. Sometimes its easier to crumble it between your fingers. (Make sure you've washed and rinsed your hands first.) **Warning! Some people are allergic to nuts so don't use groundnut oil if anyone with a nut allergy is going to eat the cous cous.**
5. Taste to check there is enough salt.

Not Rice, just Nice

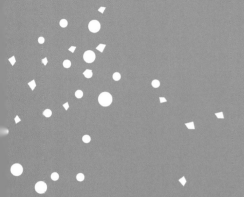

• Want to go even further? Add a handful of peanuts, almonds or pine nuts. Turn on the oven to 220°C/425°F/gas mark 7. Then sprinkle some peanuts, some almonds or some pine nuts on a baking tray. Using your oven gloves, carefully put them in the oven for about 5 minutes until they look all toasted. Keep your eye on them. Nuts have a way of going from uncooked to burnt in a second. Mix the toasted nuts through the cous cous with the raisins and onions.

Warning! Don't use any nuts if anyone with a nut allergy is going to have a taste.

• Try simply cooking the cous cous as you did on page 70 and mixing through 1-2 tablespoons of apricot jam. Sounds vile. Tastes fantastic.
• Cous cous can be eaten warm, hot or cold. You can even heat it up in the oven or in a saucepan.

Right. You've made the simplest cous cous. Now try some Easy Peasy extras and then some just as Easy Peasy dishes.

extra bites
• Peel and carefully slice 1 large onion as thinly as you can. Heat 2 tablespoons of vegetable oil in a small frying pan over a medium heat. Add the onions and some salt and cook them, stirring occasionally, until they're soft and going brown. Fork them through the cous cous when you add the oil.
• You can spice up the onions by soaking 50g of raisins in 150ml of boiling water for about 30 minutes. Drain off the water and add them to the cous cous with onions.

Green with peas

You will need 7 ingredients:

some cooked cous cous (see page 70),
   mixed through with some soft butter
   not oil
some cold water
350g of frozen peas
a big blob of butter
a teaspoon of sugar
some salt
some cinnamon

a medium saucepan with a lid
weighing scales
oven gloves
a colander in the sink
a teaspoon
a wooden spoon and a fork

1. Put a little water in the saucepan and bring it to the boil over a high heat.
2. When the water is bubbling, put the peas in and wait for them to bubble again.
3. Lower the heat, put on the lid and cook them for about 3 minutes.
4. Now, using your oven gloves, carefully take the saucepan to the sink and drain the peas in the colander. Tip them back into the saucepan and add the butter, the sugar and a little salt. Give them a stir.
5. Now use the fork to mix the buttery, sugary peas through the cous cous. Sprinkle some cinnamon over the top and eat it hot or cold.

extra bites

• If you don't like peas you could try a different vegetable, like courgettes or red peppers. Remember to wash them and cut them into small chunks first. Cook them like the peas but allow just 2 minutes for courgettes and about 5 minutes for peppers.
• If you don't like cinnamon, leave it out.

Thick & Sticky

You will need 8 ingredients:

some cooked cous cous (see page 70)
1 small onion
1 courgette
150g of ready-to-eat dried apricots
2 tablespoons of vegetable oil
1½ tablespoons of sugar
1 tablespoon of lemon juice
some cold water

a chopping board and a sharp knife
3 tablespoons
a saucepan small enough to hold the
  fruit and vegetables
a wooden spoon

1. Carefully peel and slice the onion as thinly as you can. Wash the courgette under cold, running water and slice it into small chunks.
2. Cut the apricots into small pieces.
3. Put the oil and the sugar into the saucepan and heat it on a medium heat until it turns light brown. This is called caramelising (see page 13). It takes a couple of minutes but watch it because the mixture can burn very quickly.

4. Now add the onion, the courgette, the apricots and the lemon juice.
5. Pour in enough cold water to just cover everything. Give it a good stir and let it cook on a low heat for about 1 hour until it's thick and jammy. It may need a bit longer
so keep your eye on it. Add a bit more water if it looks as if it is getting dry.
6. Mix the sauce through the cous cous – hot or cold.

extra bites

• If you like this sweet and savoury taste, try putting it in your sandwiches for lunch. Go on. Be brave!
• This is also good with cooked rice instead of cous cous.
• It's delicious with ham or cheese.

Watch out

• The trouble with caramelising (see page 13) is that it's a very hot business and you must be careful. Make extra sure that the handle of the saucepan is tucked in and away from you so you can't catch it on your sleeve or knock it off the cooker. Sugar burns are horrid. Knowing how to be careful and what to do is very important. Ask an adult for help if you haven't done this before.
• Caramelising makes the saucepan sticky and difficult to clean. When you've finished cooking, let it soak in hot, soapy water for a while before you clean it.

In your Fingers

You will need 8 ingredients:

1 pack (about 500g) of uncooked
  spare ribs
salt and pepper
2 cloves of garlic
a chunk of fresh ginger
2 tablespoons of soy sauce
2 tablespoons of tomato purée
1 tablespoon of brown sugar
1 tablespoon of groundnut or sesame oil

an ovenproof dish, big enough to hold
 the spare ribs snugly
oven gloves
a chopping board and a sharp knife
a small bowl and a wooden spoon
4 tablespoons

1. Turn on the oven to 150°C/300°F/
gas mark 2.
2. Put the spare ribs into the ovenproof
dish and sprinkle them with a little salt
and pepper.
3. Using your oven gloves, carefully put
them into the oven for 1 hour. This kind
of slow cooking is called tenderising
(see page 16).
4. Peel the garlic. Scrub the fresh ginger
under cold, running water. Chop them
both into tiny bits and put them into
the bowl.
5. Add all the rest of the ingredients to
the same bowl and mix them thoroughly.

6. Now, using your oven gloves, carefully
take the spare ribs out of the oven and put
them somewhere safe. Turn up the oven to
180°C/350°F/gas mark 4.
7. Pour the sauce over the spare ribs
making sure they're very well covered.
Using your oven gloves, carefully put them
back into the oven for 30 minutes. Check
them after 20 minutes to see how they are.
If they look cooked and crisp, take them
out of the oven. If not leave them for a
little longer.

**Warning! Don't use groundnut oil if you
have a nut allergy!**

I want it Now!

You will need 6 ingredients:

2 eggs
some caster sugar
some soft butter
some self-raising flour
2 tablespoons of drinking chocolate
   powder
some milk

a small cake tin or anything similar
some kitchen paper
a small bowl and a large bowl
weighing scales
little dishes for the sugar, butter and
   flour
a hand-held electric whisk or a wooden
   spoon
a fork and a tablespoon
oven gloves
a skewer and a wire cooling rack

1. Turn on the oven to 180°C/350°F/
gas mark 4.
2. Using kitchen paper or your fingers,
grease the cake tin and put it aside.
Remember to get into the corners.
3. Crack the eggs into the small bowl –
fish out any bits of shell – and weigh them.
4. Now, whatever the eggs weigh, weigh
out the same amount each of sugar,
butter and flour. So, if your eggs weigh
100g, for example, then weigh out 100g
of sugar, 100g of butter and 100g of flour.
5. Put the sugar and butter into the big
bowl. Beat it with the electric whisk or
the wooden spoon until it's well mixed.

6. Whisk the eggs with the fork and pour
them into the sugar and butter.
7. Now put in the flour and the drinking
chocolate powder. Mix the whole lot
together well. Then add enough milk to
make it gloopy and wet.
8. Pour the mixture into the greased cake
tin and using your oven gloves, carefully
put the cake into the oven for about
25-30 minutes.

GOOD FOR LUNCH BOXES

extra bites

There are endless things you can do with
this cake. You can:
• Peel, core and chop an apple into tiny
chunks and add it to the mixture before
it goes into the tin.
• Leave out the chocolate and eat it as
a plain cake, perhaps spread with jam.
• Cover the top with whipped cream and
some strawberries.
• Put some candles into it and sing Happy
Birthday to yourself.

Watch out

• The trouble with cakes is knowing when
they're ready. You need to test with a
skewer or something similar (see page 16).
• It's tricky getting cakes out of their tins,
but the more you do, the easier it gets.
If you're feeling a bit chicken, then ask
an adult to help. If you're OK about it,
then look at page 16 for a reminder of
what to do.

Pockets

**For 2 Pockets you will need
5 ingredients:**

100g of plain flour
1 teaspoon of baking powder
½ teaspoon of salt
60-70ml of warm water from the kettle
vegetable oil for frying

*clean hands
a large bowl and a wooden spoon
a board for rolling the dough and
   a rolling pin
a tablespoon
a small frying pan and a spatula
a wire cooling rack*

1. Put the flour, baking powder and salt into the bowl.
2. Add half the water and start to mix it with the wooden spoon. Keep adding the water until the dough is nice and firm.

3. Put some flour on your hands to stop the dough sticking to them and start pushing and folding the dough. This is called kneading. Do this for about 2 minutes. Then cut or tear it in half.
4. Sprinkle some flour onto the board and using the rolling pin, roll out one piece of the dough until it looks a bit like a pitta bread. You may prefer to do some of this with your fingertips – just gently pressing and pushing. Now do the same with the other piece.
5. Put a teaspoon of oil into the frying pan on a medium heat. Drop a tiny bit of the dough into the pan and when it starts to fizz a bit, the oil will be ready.
6. Now, carefully put one piece of the dough into the frying pan and cook it over a medium heat for about 2 minutes. Have a look at its bottom and when it's nice and golden, turn it over with the spatula and cook the other side for the same time.
7. Carefully lift it out of the frying pan with the spatula and put it on the wire cooling rack. Do exactly the same for the other one. The Pockets should be puffed and golden.
8. Let them go cold – if you can wait that long – and then slice into them with a sharp knife around three edges. Now you can fill your Pockets (see page 80)!

GOOD FOR LUNCH BOXES

What's in your Pocket?

This is where you get clever. Here's a pile of suggestions of things to do with your Pockets:

- Just eat them hot with dripping butter and runny honey.

- Mash up a banana with a tiny sprinkling of sugar and stuff it in.

- Heat some butter in a frying pan. Chop up some tomatoes, sprinkle them with salt, pepper and a dot of sugar. Fry them over a low heat, stirring occasionally, until they've gone all mushy and a little brown. When they're cold fill your Pocket with them (see page 78 for how to make them).

- Drain the juice from a small tin (80g) of tuna. Mash it with a fork together with 1 tablespoon of mayonnaise. You can even cut some cucumber or spring onion into tiny pieces and mix this in as well.

- Fill your Pocket with a pile of dressed salad (see It Could Be Lettuce on page 56). Add a little grated cheese.

- Pop in a small Cow Burglar (see page 98) and a dollop of tomato ketchup.

- Add a slice of Fowl Meat Loaf (see page 64) with some sliced tomatoes.

- Make the filling for Chopped Sandwich (see page 53) and stuff that in.

- Turn it into a BLT. Put a drop of vegetable oil into a small frying pan. When it's hot add 2 rashers of streaky bacon and cook them until they're crisp. Drain them on some kitchen paper and then pop them into your Pocket with some lettuce leaves and sliced tomatoes. You could spread a thin layer of mayonnaise or butter inside the Pocket first.

- If you want to be really wild, then fill your Pocket with one What Is This Exactly? (see page 109). Try spicing this up with a drop of Worcestershire sauce or HP sauce. OK – tomato ketchup if you must!

- Peel and core half an apple and then grate it. Mix it with 2 tablespoons of grated cheese and some mayonnaise. This is good for Pockets.

- Peel the shell from a warm, hard-boiled egg (see page 14) and put it into a bowl with a little butter, some salt and a tablespoon of Branston Pickle. Mash it all up and load your Pocket.

- Drain the oil from a tin of sardines and then mash them with a little butter, a teaspoon of nice, sweet vinegar or a squirt of lemon juice and some black pepper. Pile it into your Pocket and cover with very thin slices of cucumber.

Strips Not Chips

You will need 5 ingredients:

4-5 cold, boiled potatoes
  (see page 57)
70g of soft butter and some extra
  for greasing
75g of plain flour
1 beaten egg
some salt

a medium bowl
very clean hands and a potato masher
weighing scales
some clingfilm
a baking tray
a chopping board and a rolling pin
a small bowl for the egg and a fork
a pastry brush
a sharp knife and a spatula
oven gloves
a wire cooling rack

1. Turn on the oven to 190°C/375°F/ gas mark 5.
2. Put the cooked potatoes into the bowl and break them up with your fingers. Then give them a mash with the masher to make them a bit smoother.
3. Add the soft butter and the flour and mix it all together with your fingers as if it was a piece of bread dough.
4. When it's mixed and quite solid, wrap it in clingfilm and put it into the fridge for 30 minutes.
5. Now grease the baking tray with some butter – use your fingers or some kitchen paper. Remember to get into all the corners.

6. Sprinkle some flour onto the board and the rolling pin and roll out the mixture – any old how. You may find it easier to press out the mixture with your fingers. Flour your fingers first to stop them sticking. The mixture is quite sticky!
7. Crack the egg into the small bowl – remember to fish out any bits of shell – and whisk it.
8. Brush the surface of the potatoes with the egg (you may not use it all) and sprinkle it with salt.
9. Cut the mixture into squares and using the spatula, lift them onto the baking tray. It doesn't matter if some of them collapse. Just put them on the baking tray as well.
10. Using your oven gloves, carefully put them into the oven and cook them until they look golden and a little brown around the edges. It'll take about 15 minutes. They're just as delicious hot or cold. Let them cool on the wire cooling rack for a bit before eating them.

extra bite
• Try sprinkling some grated cheese over the top of the squares before they go into the oven.

GOOD FOR LUNCH BOXES
GOOD FOR BED

Eight for Me – None for you

You will need 4 ingredients:

325g of plain flour
100g of caster sugar
225g of soft butter
some vanilla essence

weighing scales
a mixing bowl and a wooden spoon
clean hands
a baking tray
oven gloves
a palette knife and a wire cooling rack

1. Turn on the oven to 170°C/325°F/ gas mark 3.
2. Weigh the flour, sugar and butter and put it all into the mixing bowl.
3. Add the vanilla essence and start mixing it with your wooden spoon. When it gets really sticky, use your hands (clean, please!) to squeeze the dough into a nice, smooth lump. Make sure it's very well mixed.

4. Now, pinch off pieces about the size of a large marble and roll them around in your hands into little balls. They don't have to be perfectly shaped.
5. Put them on the baking tray – not too close together because they spread a bit in the oven – and press them a bit flatter with your hand. Press very lightly.
6. Using your oven gloves, carefully put them in the oven for about 15-20 minutes until they're sandy coloured. Use your oven gloves to take them out of the oven. Put them on the wire cooling rack with the palette knife and leave them to cool. Try not to eat them straight away. Biscuits are better cold.

extra bites

• Try adding a handful of sultanas or a pile of chocolate chips to the mixture.
• Better still, let the biscuits go completely cold. Break up a couple of bars of chocolate into a saucepan. Add a little milk and let it melt slowly over a low heat. Carefully take the saucepan off the heat and dip one end of each biscuit into the melted chocolate. Put them onto a baking tray that you've covered with non-stick baking parchment and pop them into the fridge to set.

NOT GOOD FOR BED

Cracking Good Corn

You will need 3 ingredients:

2 fresh corn on the cob
25g of butter
some salt, if you want

some kitchen paper
an ovenproof dish large enough to hold
* the corn*
a little microwave dish or a saucepan
* to melt the butter in*
oven gloves

1. Turn on the oven to 170°C/325°F/
gas mark 3.
2. Prepare the corn by pulling off all the
greeny/yellowy leaves and the stringy
bits. Wash them in cold, running water
and dry them with kitchen paper. Put
them in the ovenproof dish.
3. Melt the butter either in the microwave
or on a low heat in the saucepan on the
cooker. Pour the melted butter over the
corn and roll them around until they're
well covered. Add some salt if you want.
4. Using your oven gloves, carefully put
the corn into the oven to bake and cook
for about 30 minutes until the corn is
nicely browned. Remember they'll be
very hot. Let them cool a little before
you eat them.

Watch out

• The trouble with eating corn on the cob
is that it's so difficult to hold. If you've got
little corn on the cob forks, then you're
laughing. If not, try carefully sticking an
ordinary small fork in each end. But don't
stab yourself.
• You could also wrap some kitchen paper
or foil around one end to protect your
fingers. Better still – get someone else
to hold them for you!
• Sometimes you can't get fresh corn.
Frozen corn on the cob is just as good –
especially the mini ones. But defrost them
first otherwise they'll go soggy.

Clapple

You will need 7 ingredients:

110g of soft butter and some extra for
    greasing the tin
2 eggs
the rind from 1 lemon
2 apples
110g of caster sugar
175g of self-raising flour
some milk

some kitchen paper
a 450g (1lb) non-stick loaf tin
a small bowl for the eggs
a lemon zester
a chopping board and a sharp knife
weighing scales and a mixing bowl
a wooden spoon or a hand-held electric
  whisk
some greaseproof paper
a skewer and a wire cooling rack

1. Turn on the oven to 180°C/350°F/
gas mark 4.
2. Using the kitchen paper or your
fingers, grease the loaf tin, remembering
to get into the corners.
3. Crack the eggs into the small bowl –
fish out any bits of shell.
4. Now using the zester, carefully remove
the rind from the lemon (see page 11 for
how to do this).
5. Wash, peel and core the apples. Chop
them into tiny chunks.

6. Now weigh out the rest of the
ingredients. Put them in the bowl with
the eggs and mix them thoroughly with
the electric whisk or the wooden spoon.
7. Mix in the apples with the wooden
spoon. If the mixture is very thick and
sticky, pour in a little milk.
8. Tip the whole lot into the loaf tin. Put
a piece of greaseproof paper over the top
and using your oven gloves, carefully put
the tin into the oven. To test whether the
cake is cooked, take it out of the oven
using your oven gloves and put it
somewhere safe. Push the skewer into the
middle and pull it out. If the cake is cooked
the skewer will be clean. If not pop the
loaf tin back into the oven for another
5-10 minutes.
9. When it's cooked, let the Clapple cool in
the tin for a few minutes before tipping it
out onto the cooling rack. See page 16 for
how to tip out a cake (or ask for help if you
need it). Let the cake cool before eating it.

extra bites
• Try adding a teaspoon of cinnamon to
the mixture.
• Cut a slice and spread a little butter on
it. But don't tell anyone!

GOOD FOR LUNCH BOXES

Yum - Egg Whites!

Warning! This needs lots of hours in the oven, so make sure no one's going to be using it but you.

You will need 2 ingredients:

3 egg whites
175g of caster sugar

a large baking tray
scissors and non-stick baking
  parchment or greaseproof paper
weighing scales
a large mixing bowl (metal if you've
  got one)
a hand-held electric whisk
a metal spoon
oven gloves

1. Turn on the oven to 140°C/275°F/ gas mark 1.
2. With the scissors, cut a piece of baking parchment or greaseproof paper to cover the bottom of the baking tray.
3. Put the egg whites into the bowl and, using the hand-held electric whisk, whisk them until they're really stiff. It's hard work but keep going. Experiment by tipping the bowl upside down. If the whites are stiff enough, they won't fall out – really!

4. Now sprinkle a spoonful of sugar over the surface of the egg whites and whisk again until the sugar disappears. Keep doing this until all the sugar has been whisked in. The meringue mixture should look shiny by now.
5. Spoon out large dollops of meringue onto the baking tray. They can be any size you like. But the bigger the better. Leave a little space between each one to let them breathe while they're cooking.
6. Using your oven gloves, carefully put the meringues into the oven for 3-4 hours. Turn off the oven and leave the meringues to dry out – overnight, if possible.
7. The next morning have a meringue for breakfast. No don't!

extra bites

• Meringues are gorgeous just on their own – especially for break or in your lunch box.
• Try whisking some double cream until it's nice and thick and use it as a filling between two huge meringues.
• Crumble them up and mix them up with soft ice-cream and fresh raspberries.
• Serve them with fresh strawberries or raspberries and cream.
• Plop on a pile of whipped cream with a few mini chocolate eggs on top. Then sit on them until they hatch!

GOOD FOR LUNCH BOXES

on the Table

When my boys come home from school they have a snack, do their homework and watch telly. That's how it is most days in our house. But all they really want is supper. 'Mum, when will supper be ready?' they moan. 'Mum, what's for supper?' they demand. 'Aw Mum, we had that last night,' they whine.

Have you ever noticed that whatever you have for your snack after school you're still starving? One of the reasons could be that snacking is never quite satisfying enough. What your body really needs is a meal, like supper, for example. Supper is a bit like a full stop – not the kind at the end of a sentence but the kind that means 'this is the end of my day'. And usually it's been long and tiring. Sometimes you're just plum tuckered out from sport and need some fresh energy. That's why supper is such a good meal. Try to have it every day.

There's no reason why you can't make it yourself for you and anyone else who's around. If you're like my boys and moan about food, then why don't you choose what you want to eat, ask an adult if it's OK and then make it. There's usually time to cook after school and before you have to go to bed. And if it happens to be a particularly good telly night, or you've got lots of homework, then leave it until the weekend. But have a go!

interesting fact
Can't think of any. Can you?

Hold on a minute!

- Remember to be prepared. **Get everything ready** before you start. That means **washing your hands** as well!

- Remember that if you don't understand something or haven't done it before, look back to **Easy Peasy How to do Everything All the Time** on page 10 or **Pots and Pans and Things** on page 22.

- Remember only use **sharp knives**. Blunt ones can be dangerous. Take care when you're using them.

- Remember to use your **oven gloves** when something is hot.

- Remember to **turn off the oven, cooker or grill** when you've finished cooking.

- Remember to **enjoy yourself** and to **ask for help** if you need it.

on the Table

92 **RED 'N' YELLOW**

94 **SOME OF US LIKE FISH**

96 **ONE SAUCE**

97 **BALLS – WITH ONE SAUCE!**

98 **DO YOU LIKE MUSHROOMS?**

100 **LETUSPEA STEW**

101 **SCRUMPTIOUS BEANS**

102 **PIGS AND RICE – VERY NICE**

104 **OVEN LEGS**

105 **NO PASTRY PIE**

106 **COW BURGLARS**

108 **FISHING FOR EGGS**

109 **WHAT IS THIS EXACTLY?**

110 **FAB PRAWNS**

112 **VERI QUICKI SPAGHETTI**

114 **SUCH A SWEETIE**

115 **FOOLED YOU!**

116 **B & B**

118 **PEARS FOR PUDDING**

Red 'n' Yellow

You will need 6 ingredients:

100g of mushrooms
1 small onion
1 red pepper
2 blobs of butter
4 eggs
some salt

some kitchen paper
a vegetable chopping board
  and a sharp knife
a medium frying pan
a wooden spoon
a small bowl and a fork

1. Clean the mushrooms with some damp kitchen paper. Take a thin slice off their bottoms and chop them up any old how.
2. Peel the onion and carefully slice it as thinly as you can.
3. Wash the pepper under cold, running water. Chop off its stalk, pull it apart and scrape out the little white seeds and pithy bits. Slice it as thinly as you can.

4. Put a blob of butter in the frying pan over a medium heat and when it starts to sizzle add the mushrooms. Stir them around and let them cook until they're soft.
5. Now add another blob of butter and when that's sizzling add the onion, pepper and a good pinch of salt. Mix it up thoroughly and let it cook, stirring occasionally, until the onions go very soft and change colour. This will take about 10-15 minutes depending on how thick you've cut the vegetables.
6. Crack the eggs into the bowl – remember to fish out any bits of shell – and whisk them with the fork.
7. Pour them into the frying pan and keep stirring until the eggs are cooked enough for you – about 2-3 minutes is a good guide.

extra bite
• This is especially good with hot, buttered toast and a glass of milk.

Watch out
• Eggs go on cooking for a while after you've taken them off the heat. So it's best to eat them straight away before they turn into yellow rocks!
• The trouble with cooking eggs like this is the mess they leave in the frying pan. When you've finished cooking, put the pan somewhere safe to cool down for a bit. Then let it soak in hot, soapy water before you clean it.

Some of us Like Fish

You will need 5 ingredients:

2 slices of dry bread for breadcrumbs
  (see page 15)
some grated cheese
some butter
2 fillets of white fish (haddock, lemon
  sole or cod)
some salt and pepper

a liquidiser or a food processor
a small bowl
a tablespoon
an ovenproof dish small enough to hold
  the fish snugly
some kitchen paper
a chopping board and a sharp knife
oven gloves

1. Turn on the oven to 190°C/375°F/
gas mark 5.
2. Make the breadcrumbs first (see page
15) and tip them into the small bowl.
3. Add 4 tablespoons of grated cheese to
the breadcrumbs and mix them together.
4. Now grease the ovenproof dish with lots
of butter. You can use some kitchen paper
or your fingers (make sure they're clean!).
5. Wash the fish under cold, running water
and pat it dry with kitchen paper. Put it onto
the board and press it all over with your
fingers to make sure there are no bones.
If you find any, cut them out with a sharp
knife or pull them out with your fingers.
6. Put the fish into the ovenproof dish
and sprinkle it with a little salt and pepper.
7. Sprinkle over the cheesy breadcrumbs
and add an extra sprinkling of cheese over
the top.
8. Now, using your oven gloves, put the dish
into the oven for about 20-25 minutes.

extra bites

• If you want this a bit juicier, try melting a
little butter and mixing it in with the cheesy
breadcrumbs.
• This is very nice with peas and little,
boiled potatoes (see page 57) or a salad
(see page 56).
• You don't have to use all the same fish.
Try a combination of salmon and sole or
haddock and cod.
• Chop up some fresh coriander and mix
it in with the cheesy breadcrumbs.

One Sauce

You will need 5 ingredients:

1 onion
2 cloves of garlic
2-3 tablespoons of olive oil
1 can (400g) of chopped tomatoes
some salt and black pepper

a chopping board and a sharp knife
a tablespoon
a medium saucepan with a lid
a tin opener
a wooden spoon and a hand-held
  electric blender

1. Peel and carefully chop the onions and garlic as finely as you can.
2. Add the oil to the saucepan and warm it over a medium heat. Add the onions and garlic and stir them around until they're well coated with the oil.
3. Now, lower the heat and leave the onions to cook for about 15 minutes, stirring occasionally to stop them burning.
4. Turn up the heat, tip in the tomatoes and add 2-3 good pinches of salt and some black pepper. Give it a good stir. When it starts to bubble a little, lower the heat right down, put the lid on and leave it cook for about 25 minutes. Stir it occasionally.
5. Now, take off the lid and let it cook for another 20 minutes, stirring occasionally, on a very low heat.

6. Let the sauce cool a little and then taste it. Add a little more salt if you like. If you want a smooth sauce give it a quick whiz with the hand-held electric blender.

Watch out
• The trouble with One Sauce is that there are so many things to do with it. Here are some ideas.

What to do with One Sauce
• Wait for it to cool down and eat it straight from the saucepan.
• Dip into it some bread, toast or bread sticks (see page 66).
• Mix it through some freshly cooked spaghetti (see page 112) with a sprinkling of Parmesan cheese on top.
• Use it as the topping for a pizza.
• Slice a baguette in half and pull out a little of the soft white bread. Spread some One Sauce on it and sprinkle with a pile of grated cheese and some black pepper. Put it under the grill until the cheese melts and looks a bit brown and bubbly.
• Or turn it into . . . Balls – With One Sauce! (see page 97).

Balls – with One Sauce!

You will need 2 ingredients:

One Sauce (see page 96)
Balls First (see page 62)

*a saucepan with a lid, big enough to hold
   the Balls easily
a wooden spoon*

1. Put the Balls First into the saucepan and pour over the One Sauce.
2. Put the pan on the cooker on a medium heat until the sauce starts to look a bit fizzy and bubbly on the top.
3. Now, lower the heat right down, put on the lid and let it all cook slowly for about 20 minutes.
4. Take a look at it every now and then to make sure it's still juicy. Give the Balls a little poke occasionally. You can always add a little water to juice it up a bit.

Do You like Mushrooms?

You will need 9 ingredients:

1 small onion
2 cloves of garlic
a large blob of butter
250g of mushrooms
350g of rice
1 vegetable stock cube dissolved in
   600ml of boiling water
a large handful of chopped, fresh
parsley
some salt and pepper
lots of grated Parmesan cheese

a chopping board and a sharp knife
a medium saucepan with a lid
a wooden spoon
weighing scales
some kitchen paper
a heatproof measuring jug and a kettle
   of boiling water

1. Peel and chop the onion and garlic into tiny bits.
2. Melt the butter in the saucepan over a low heat. When it starts to fizz a little, add the onion and garlic and stir them around with the wooden spoon. Let them cook very slowly until they're soft. It'll take about 15 minutes.
3. Clean the mushrooms with some damp kitchen paper and take a thin slice off the bottom of the stalks. Throw the bottoms away. Slice the mushrooms up any old how but not too thick.
4. Add them to the saucepan. Turn up the heat and let them cook, stirring occasionally, until they get nice and juicy.
5. Add the rice and mix it all together with the wooden spoon.
6. Pour in the stock with some salt and pepper. When it starts to bubble, lower the heat right down, put on the lid and let it cook gently for 25-30 minutes, stirring it often. It can dry up very quickly so add some hot water from the kettle if this happens.
7. Add the chopped, fresh parsley and taste it. You may want to add a little more salt or pepper.
8. Serve this with lots of freshly grated Parmesan cheese.

extra bite
• You could add some little pieces or strips of ham if you fancy.

Letuspea Stew

You will need 7 ingredients:

half an iceberg lettuce
200g of frozen peas
1 tablespoon of water or vegetable stock
25g of butter
2 egg yolks
some salt and pepper
some thin strips of ham

a medium saucepan with a lid
weighing scales
a tablespoon
2 small bowls for the eggs
a fork and a wooden spoon

1. Wash the lettuce under cold, running water. Tear it up into very small pieces. This is called shredding (see page 16). Put it into the saucepan with the peas, the water and the butter.
2. Put the saucepan on the cooker on a high heat. When it starts to get hot – you'll hear a fizzing noise and it'll get a bit steamy – put the lid on and turn the heat very low. Leave it for 15 minutes.
3. While the lettuce is cooking, separate the eggs (see page 10 for how to do this). Whisk the yolks with the fork and season them with salt and pepper.
4. Now tip the egg yolks and ham into the saucepan and stir it all around until it gets nice and thick. It should take about 5 minutes. Taste it and add some more salt and pepper if you want.

extra bite
• What are you going to do with those left-over egg whites? Use them to make meringues (see page 86) or throw them away.

Scrumptious Beans

You will need 11 ingredients:

1 red pepper
1 large clove of garlic
1 onion
3-4 tablespoons of olive oil
a big handful of mushrooms
1 can (400g) of red kidney beans
1 can (400g) of tomatoes
2 tablespoons of sultanas
1 teaspoon of mild curry powder or paste
2 tablespoons of mango chutney
a good pinch of salt and plenty of black
   pepper

a chopping board and a sharp knife
a medium saucepan with a lid
a wooden spoon
some kitchen paper
a tin opener and a colander in the sink
2 tablespoons and a teaspoon

1. Wash the pepper in cold, running water. Cut off its stalk and pull apart. Scrape out the seeds and any white, pithy bits. Slice it into small chunks.
2. Peel the garlic and onion and chop them into little chunks.
3. Heat the oil in the saucepan on a medium heat. Drop in a tiny piece of onion and when it starts to sizzle, add the rest of the onion, the garlic and the pepper.

4. Stir it around with the wooden spoon and let it cook for about 10 minutes, stirring occasionally to stop the vegetables sticking to the bottom of the saucepan.
5. Prepare the mushrooms by cutting a thin slice off the bottom of the stalks and wiping them over with some damp kitchen paper. Then chop them any old how.
6. Rinse the kidney beans in the colander under cold, running water. Give them a shake.
7. Now add the beans, the mushrooms and everything else. Give it all a good stir and when it starts to look very hot, turn the heat right down. Put on the lid and let it cook very slowly for about 1 hour, stirring occasionally.
8. Serve Scrumptious Beans with crusty bread and a nice, crisp salad.

extra bites
• If you hate kidney beans you can use butter beans or cannellini beans.
• This is just as delicious hot or cold and seems to taste better the next day.

Pigs and Rice – very nice

You will need 7 ingredients:

1 large pepper (any colour)
1 large onion
2 tablespoons of olive oil
4 pork chops (loin chops are nicest)
4 tablespoons of uncooked rice
1 can (400g) of tomatoes
some salt and pepper

a chopping board and a sharp knife
2 tablespoons
*a casserole dish you can use on
   the cooker*
*a wooden spoon and a pair of
   kitchen tongs*
a can opener
oven gloves

1. Turn on the oven to 190°C/375°F/
gas mark 5.
2. Wash the pepper in cold, running
water. Cut off its stalk and pull it apart.
Scrape out the seeds and any white,
pithy bits.
3. Peel the onion and slice it with the
peppers as thinly as you can.

4. Heat the oil in the casserole over a
medium heat. Drop in a tiny piece of onion
and when it sizzles add all the onion and
the pepper slices. Turn them over in the oil
and cook them for about 8-10 minutes,
stirring often. They should be soft and
sweet smelling.
5. Now, with a sharp knife, carefully cut
off any large pieces of fat from the chops.
Turn the heat up high and put them into
the casserole.
6. Let them cook for about 2 minutes and
then, using the tongs, carefully turn them
over and cook the other side for another
2 minutes.
7. Lower the heat and add the rice,
tomatoes and some salt and pepper. Give
it all a good mix with the wooden spoon.
8. Put the lid on the casserole and using
your oven gloves, carefully put it into the
oven and let it cook for about 45 minutes.
Check it after 30 minutes and add some
water if it looks a bit dry. (You may need
some adult help for this.)

extra bites
• Try adding a large handful of chopped,
fresh sage.
• If you're not sure about using the tongs,
then cook this with cubes of pork instead
of chops. Then you won't have to turn
anything over. You'll just need a wooden
spoon.

oven Legs

You will need 3 ingredients:

6 or 8 chicken drumsticks
1 small onion
some salt

a roasting tin or an ovenproof dish
a chopping board and a sharp knife
oven gloves

1. Turn on the oven to 220°C/425°F/
gas mark 7.
2. Put the drumsticks into the roasting
tin (or ovenproof dish) and sprinkle
them with salt. They need quite a bit.
3. Peel and slice the onion as thinly as
you can. Sprinkle it over the chicken.
4. Using your oven gloves, carefully
put the tin into the oven and cook the
drumsticks for about 1 hour until
they're crisp on the outside.
5. Using your oven gloves, take the
drumsticks out of the oven and eat
them in your fingers. Remember they'll
be hot so you may have to start with a
knife
and fork.

GOOD FOR A SNACK

extra bite
• You might like to try roasting some tiny
potato cubes with the chicken. Peel 2
baking potatoes. Then wash them, dry
them with some kitchen paper and cut
them into very small cubes, about the size
of large dice. Put the potato cubes into a
bowl and add some salt and a tablespoon
of olive oil.
Mix them around and tip them into the
roasting tin with the chicken drumsticks.

No pastry pie

You will need 8 ingredients:

4-5 boiled potatoes (see page 57)
some milk
a little butter
2 eggs
a handful of fresh parsley
1-2 handfuls of grated cheese
1 can (400g) of tomatoes
some salt and pepper

a large bowl and a small bowl
a potato masher and a fork
some kitchen paper
a chopping board and a sharp knife
a tin opener
a wooden spoon
oven gloves and an ovenproof dish

1. Turn on the oven to 180°C/350°F/ gas mark 4.
2. Put the potatoes in the large bowl. Add some milk and a little butter and mash them with the masher until they're soft.
3. Crack the eggs into the little bowl – remember to fish out any bits of shell – and whisk them with the fork. Add them to the potatoes.
4. Wash the parsley and dry it in the kitchen paper. Take off (and throw away) any thick, woody stems and chop up the leaves as small as you can.
5. Now put the chopped, fresh parsley, the grated cheese and the tomatoes into the potatoes and eggs. Sprinkle with some salt and pepper.
6. Mix it all very thoroughly with the wooden spoon and pile it into the ovenproof dish. Sprinkle some extra cheese over the top.
7. Using your oven gloves, carefully put the dish into the oven and bake it for about 40 minutes.

Cow Burglars

You will need 7 ingredients:

half a small onion
a large clove of garlic
225g of minced beef
50g of breadcrumbs (see page 15)
a blob of tomato ketchup (if you like
   ketchup)
1 dessertspoon of Worcestershire sauce
some salt and pepper

clean hands
a chopping board and a sharp knife
a medium bowl
a dessertspoon
a grill and a grill pan with a rack
some kitchen tongs

1. Turn on the grill. (Ask for help if you need it.)
2. Peel and carefully chop the onion and garlic as finely as you can. If you've got a food processor, do it in that. Put the chopped onion and garlic into the bowl.
3. Put everything else into the bowl and mix it all together very well with your clean hands. Hands are best to make sure everything is properly mixed. Do a fair bit of squeezing and mixing. The more you do, the smoother the mixture. This makes burgering very easy.
4. Take a small handful of the mixture. Mould it into a burger shape and put it on the chopping board. Keep doing this until all the mixture is used up. You should get about 4 Burglars.

5. Now put them onto the grill rack and grill them for about 6-7 minutes on each side. If you've made big, thick ones, cook them for about 8 minutes each side. Turn them over very carefully with the kitchen tongs and watch out for hot, spitting fat.
6. To check they're cooked all the way through, cut the biggest Burglar in half. If the meat still looks pink then pop them back under the grill for a few more minutes.

extra bites
• Try making Cow Burglars with minced lamb instead of beef.
• Leave out the Worcestershire sauce and add a teaspoon of curry powder to the meat before you mix it.
• Try serving them with some One Sauce (see page 96).
• When you're serving your Cow Burglars, try putting them all onto a large serving plate or wooden board and add a few sprigs of fresh parsley to make them look extra good. Then put a pile of round bread rolls into a bowl and fill a little dish with tomato ketchup or HP sauce. Let everyone make their own Burglars. A large bowl of chips would do nicely as well!

Watch out
• The trouble with grilling is the grill pan always gets so dirty. You can save yourself a lot of washing up by lining the grill pan with some kitchen foil before cooking on it. That way you can just scrumple up the foil and throw it away at the end.

Fishing for Eggs

You will need 5 ingredients:

2 small fillets of smoked haddock
a little pepper
a blob of butter
about 150ml of milk
2 eggs

a chopping board and a sharp knife
some kitchen paper
a small saucepan with a lid
a measuring jug
oven gloves
a small bowl and a fork
a wooden spoon

1. Put the fish on the board and press it all over with your fingers to make sure there are no bones. If you find any, cut them out with the knife or pull them out with your fingers. It doesn't matter if the fish breaks.

2. Wash the fish in cold, running water and pat it dry with the kitchen paper. Put it into the saucepan. If it doesn't fit, cut it up.

3. Add a little pepper, a blob of butter and the milk.

4. Put the saucepan on the cooker on a high heat until the milk starts to fizz gently around the edges. Now lower the heat right down, put the lid on and leave it for 7-8 minutes until the fish is soft and flaky. Milk has a way of boiling over quickly. So watch it and if it looks like happening, lift the lid a little to let some air in.

5. When it's ready, use your oven gloves and take the saucepan off the heat. Put it somewhere safe and poke it a bit with the sharp knife to break it up. You may want to take out any bits of black skin.

6. Now, crack the eggs into the bowl – remember to fish out any bits of shell – and whisk them with the fork.

7. Put the saucepan back onto the cooker and tip in the eggs. Stir them all around on a medium heat until the eggs are cooked – yellowy and just beginning to firm up.

8. Eat this warm with piles of hot, buttery toast.

Watch out

• The trouble with cooking eggs like this is the mess they leave in the saucepan. When you've finished cooking, put the saucepan somewhere safe to cool down for a bit. Then leave it to soak in hot, soapy water.

• Eggs go on cooking for a while after you've taken them off the heat. So it's best to eat them straight away before they turn into yellow rocks!

What is this Exactly?

You will need 5 ingredients:

1 small onion
2 tablespoons of vegetable oil
200g of minced beef
some salt and pepper
4 eggs

a chopping board and a sharp knife
a frying pan
a tablespoon and a wooden spoon
oven gloves
a medium bowl
a small bowl and a fork
a soup ladle and a spatula

1. Peel and chop the onion into small pieces.
2. Put the oil into the frying pan and let it warm on a medium heat. Drop in a piece of onion and when it starts to fizz, add all the rest. Cook this, stirring occasionally, until the onion gets goldeny-brown.
3. Now turn the heat up high and add the minced beef with a little salt and pepper. Keep turning it all over with the spoon. When the meat changes colour, lower the heat and cook it, stirring occasionally, for 7-8 minutes.
4. Now, using your oven gloves, carefully take the pan off the heat and tip it into the medium bowl. Let it cool a bit.
5. In the small bowl, crack the eggs – remember to fish out any bits of shell – and whisk them with the fork. Tip them into the meat mixture and mix it well.
6. Put the frying pan back onto the cooker. Add a little more oil if the pan looks dry and heat it over a medium heat until it looks a bit shimmery and shiny.
7. Pour a soup ladle of the mixture into the frying pan. Let it cook for a couple of minutes and when its bottom is nice and brown, carefully turn it over using the spatula. Let the other side cook for another minute or so.

extra bites

• You can eat these hot or cold. So if you don't scoff them all, keep 1 or 2 for your school lunch box.
• They're great with tomato ketchup or brown sauce – especially if you eat them cold.
• Try adding a handful of chopped, fresh parsley into the mixture.
• You could even add a tomato, chopped into small chunks and cooked first with the meat.

Fab Prawns

You will need 7 ingredients:

2 green peppers
a chunk of fresh ginger (about the size
    of a baby's little finger), washed and
    thinly sliced
2 tablespoons of olive oil
300g of cooked prawns
2 tablespoons of tomato ketchup
some salt and pepper
1 tablespoon of Worcestershire sauce

a chopping board and a sharp knife
a large frying pan or a wok
a wooden spoon
a tablespoon

1. Wash the peppers in cold, running water.
Chop off their stalks, pull them apart and
take out the seeds and white pithy bits with
your fingers. Chop them up any old how but
not too big.
2. Heat the oil over a high heat in the frying
pan. When it starts to look all shimmery,
carefully tip in the peppers and the ginger.
Stir them around with the wooden spoon.
Lower the heat a little and cook them for
about 10 minutes. Keep stirring so they
don't burn.
3. Now add all the other ingredients and
cook them for another 10 minutes or so.
Keep turning it all over with the wooden
spoon.

extra bite
• I hate to say this but Fab Prawns are
very good with brown rice. Really. You
need something like rice to mop up all
the ketchup. And as you know, prawns
and rice are very nice!

Veri Quicki Spaghetti

**For each person you will need
5 ingredients:**

cold water
some salt
100g of dried spaghetti
a blob of butter
some grated cheese

*weighing scales
a large saucepan
a teaspoon
a long-handled spoon and a fork
oven gloves
a colander in the sink
a serving bowl*

1. Fill the saucepan three-quarters full with cold water. Add about 4 teaspoons of salt and taste it. It needs to be quite salty.
2. Put the saucepan on the cooker and bring the water to the boil over a high heat.
3. When it's bubbling fiercely, carefully add the pasta and stir it in with the long-handled spoon until it's all under water. Be careful of the steam.

4. Check the packet for cooking times. Most pastas take between 4 and 12 minutes. When it's cooked, use the fork to carefully pull out a bit and taste it. Remember it'll be very hot. If it seems too hard, cook it for another minute. Keep testing until the spaghetti is cooked and has a nice bite to it.
5. Using the oven gloves, carefully take the saucepan to the sink and drain the spaghetti into the colander. Then tip it back into the saucepan. Ask for adult help if you need it.
6. Now add a large blob of butter and mix it thoroughly. Carefully tip the spaghetti into your bowl and sprinkle plenty of cheese on top. Eat it straight away. Spaghetti doesn't like waiting!

extra bites
• Instead of adding butter and cheese, try adding a tablespoon of olive oil and a crushed clove of garlic. Make sure it's well mixed through and very hot when you tip it into your bowl.
• Try sprinkling some freshly chopped herbs over your spaghetti – some fresh parsley, coriander or basil.
• While the spaghetti is draining you could melt some butter or heat a little oil and then add some freshly chopped tomatoes and basil. They'll need to cook for 5 minutes in the butter before you tip the spaghetti back into the saucepan. Once again, make sure the spaghetti is nice and hot when it gets to the bowl.

Such a Sweetie

You will need 5 ingredients:

4 chicken thighs
some salt and pepper
half a lemon
5 tablespoons of runny honey
a blob of butter

an ovenproof dish small enough to hold
the chicken thighs snugly
a lemon squeezer or your hands
a tablespoon
a small saucepan or a microwave dish
a wooden spoon
clingfilm or kitchen foil
oven gloves

1. Put the thighs into the ovenproof dish and sprinkle them with some salt and pepper.
2. Using the lemon squeezer or your hands, squeeze the lemon juice over the thighs.
3. Put the honey and the butter into the saucepan and melt them over a low heat on the cooker. Or you can do this in the microwave in the microwave dish. Carefully pour the mixture over the thighs.
4. When it's cooled down, cover the dish with clingfilm or kitchen foil and put it into the fridge for an hour to soak up the juices. This is called marinating (see page 15).
5. After half an hour or so, turn on the oven to 220°C/425°F/gas mark 7. This will get the oven hot enough while the thighs marinate for the last 30 minutes.

6. Take off the clingfilm or foil and carefully using your oven gloves, put the chicken into the oven for 30 minutes.
7. Now lower the temperature to 190°C/375°F/gas mark 5 and let the chicken roast for another 30 minutes. When the chicken is ready, take it carefully out of the oven.

extra bites

• This is delicious served with little, boiled potatoes (see page 57) and a salad (see page 56) or some peas.
• Try letting the thighs go cold and then tearing the chicken into strips to have in a sandwich with some tomato, lettuce and mayonnaise.
• Have you ever tried fried chicken and bananas? Once you've torn the cold chicken into strips, heat a little butter in a small frying pan over a medium heat. When it sizzles, put the chicken in and stir it around. After a few minutes, unzip a banana, slice it and add it to the frying pan. Cook until the banana starts to go brown.

Watch out

• The trouble with lemon pips is they always get into places they shouldn't. Either squeeze the lemon and then sieve it or simply fish out the pips with a teaspoon. You choose.

Fooled You!

You will need 3 ingredients:

500g of raspberries
3 tablespoons of caster sugar
275ml of double or whipping cream

weighing scales and a sieve
a liquidiser or a food processor
a large bowl for the cream
a tablespoon
a hand-held electric whisk
clingfilm

1. Wash the raspberries under cold, running water in the sieve. Put them into the liquidiser or processor and whiz for a few seconds.
2. Pour the cream into the large bowl and whip it with the electric whisk until it gets very stiff and sticks up like your hair first thing in the morning.
3. Now carefully, a bit at a time, fold the raspberries and the sugar into the cream (see page 14).
4. Cover the fool with clingfilm and let it chill in the fridge. Don't leave it all day before eating it. It'll only stay stiff for a few hours.

extra bites
• Try making this with strawberries, peaches, kiwis or mangoes. Remember to wash any fruit that doesn't get peeled first.
• If you hate raspberry pips you can always pour the whizzed raspberries through a sieve before adding them to the cream.

GOOD FOR FRIENDS

B & B

You will need 6 ingredients:

some soft butter for greasing
4 tablespoons of apricot jam
4 large (not too ripe) bananas
2 tablespoons of brown sugar
3-4 slices of white bread
100g of melted butter

*an ovenproof dish large enough to hold
    the bananas
some kitchen paper
a small saucepan or a microwave dish
2 tablespoons
a chopping board and a knife
weighing scales
oven gloves*

1. Turn on the oven to 190°C/375°F/
gas mark 5.
2. Grease the inside of the ovenproof dish
with some soft butter using kitchen paper
or your fingers (clean ones, please!).
3. Peel and slice the bananas quite thinly
and put them into the dish.

4. Put the jam into the saucepan and warm
it over a low heat until it's runny. Or you
can do this in the microwave in the
microwave dish. Pour the runny jam over
the bananas and sprinkle the sugar on top.
5. Cut the crusts off the bread and cut it
into squares or triangles. Melt the butter in
the same way that you melted the jam. You
can even use the same saucepan or dish.
6. Dip the bread into the melted butter
and lay the pieces over the bananas.
Try to cover up and hide all the banana.
7. Sprinkle over a bit more sugar and, using
your oven gloves, carefully pop them into
the oven for about 30 minutes until the
bread is crisp and golden. Serve B & B
with cream or ice-cream.

extra bites
• Try sprinkling a handful of poppy seeds
over the bananas.
• If you're not keen on bananas, make this
with pears or apples. You'll need to wash,
peel and core them. Then slice them thinly.
These fruit are not as sweet as bananas
so you may want to add some extra sugar
or jam. Experiment!

Watch out
• The trouble with puddings like these is
that they're just as good hot or cold. So
you can have your pudding hot and then
finish it off cold while you're helping with
the washing up.

pears for pudding

You will need 5 ingredients:

3 large pears
3 tablespoons of golden syrup
150ml of water
100g of breadcrumbs (see page 15)
60g of butter

a vegetable peeler
an ovenproof dish small enough to hold
  the pears snugly
a measuring jug
a small saucepan or a microwave dish
  to melt the butter in
a little spoon and a palette knife
oven gloves
a sharp knife or a skewer

1. Turn on the oven to 170°C/325°F/ gas mark 3.
2. Wash the pears in cold, running water. Peel them with a vegetable peeler and then cut them into quarters. Scoop out their pips.
3. Put them into the ovenproof dish and pour the syrup and water over them.
4. Melt the butter on a low heat in the saucepan or using the microwave and mix it into the breadcrumbs.
5. Spread the mixture over the top of the pears with the palette knife.
6. Using your oven gloves, carefully put the dish into the oven and bake for about 1½ hours. To test whether the pears are cooked, take the dish out of the oven using your oven gloves and put it somewhere safe. Push the tip of the knife or a skewer into one pear. If it's still hard then put the pears back in the oven for another 10 minutes.
7. Serve the pears hot with cream, a large dollop of ice-cream or just on their own.

How to live Long enough to eat your next meal

STAY CLEAN . . .

- Always cook with **clean hands**. Wash them with **soap** before you start cooking and again at the end. Just imagine what might go into your food after you've scratched your head or picked your nose!
- If you absolutely must put things back in the saucepan after you've **dropped them on the floor**, then wash them first under cold, running water. If you can't remember when **you** last washed the kitchen floor (HA! HA!), then throw it in the bin.
- Think about wearing a **pinnie** if you don't want to change your clothes every time you whisk an egg! At least **roll up your sleeves** or wear **short sleeves**, so they don't get in the way.

- Please use different **chopping boards** for different foods so you don't help any nasty little **bugs** travel from one to the other. This is especially important for meats and vegetables. Most of us only have a couple of boards at home. So do your best. Just make sure they're very clean and that you don't use **cooked foods** on the same boards as **raw foods**.
- The same applies to **knives**. Keep them separate or wash them with hot, soapy water and dry them carefully between jobs.
- Use clean towels, clean cloths and clean work surfaces. Just imagine what might be getting cosy in the **cracks** between the tiles on your work surface, especially if the **cat** has just walked over them. Imagine what could be nestling in the fibres of the washing-up cloth. And think what could be having fun in the sponge. And by the way, they need to be clean when you've finished as well. I know – nag, nag, nag.

STAY SHARP . . .

- Use **sharp knives**. They're a lot safer than blunt ones. The blunter a knife is the more likely it is to slip when you're trying to cut something. If you use a sharp knife that's small and comfortable in your hand, you'll do the job better. Always use knives very carefully. You don't want bits of finger in the food.
- **Concentrate** on what you're doing if you want to avoid cutting your finger off. When you're chopping vegetables keep your **fingers tucked in**. Sometimes it's helpful to spear the vegetable with a fork and hold the fork with one hand while you cut with the other one.
- Always keep plasters in the kitchen as **cuts hurt** a lot and they give you a fright. If you do cut yourself, wash the cut under **cold, running water**, dry it and put a plaster on. If the cut is a bad one, wrap it up tightly in a clean towel and call an adult.
- Take care when you're **washing the blades** from your food processor or taking it to pieces after you've used it. The blades are very sharp – that's why they do such a good job.

STAY COOL . . .

- Always use cold water from the **cold tap**, letting it run a bit first. Hot water should come from a **boiled kettle**. Hot tap water is normally stored in a tank somewhere in your house which means it's a bit stale by the time it comes out of the tap. Boiling it makes it safe to use.
- Remember that **boiling water can burn you**. Not just the water itself but the steam that comes off it. Have you ever noticed how much steam comes out of a kettle or from underneath the lid of a saucepan? Opening the oven door when the oven is hot is exactly the same. Be careful and **stand back** to let the steam blow away.
- Remember that **if you wear glasses** they'll steam up as well and that can be dangerous.
- Don't get too close to the **gas burner** when you switch on. Sometimes there's a delay between turning on the gas and it actually lighting. When that happens there's often a **burst of flame** that comes as a bit of a shock. The same applies to the grill – be careful of your hands, arms, face and hair.
- If you do burn yourself, run the burnt bit under cold, running water for at least **10 minutes**. The water must be very cold to help take the sting out of the burn. Always call an adult.

- Remember that there are lots of ways you can burn yourself in the kitchen. **Here are some golden rules**:
- **Never** leave the handle of a saucepan sticking out.
- **Never** leave a cooking spoon in the pan while something's cooking.
- **Try** to use long-handled spoons or spatulas for cooking hot things.
- **Always** use oven gloves to handle hot things.
- **Always** put hot things somewhere safe and out of the way.
- **Always** be careful when frying as hot fat can spit.
- Remember that **water** and **electricity** do not mix. If you unplug or switch off an electric socket with **wet hands**, you'll probably get an **electric shock**. And they are very nasty. Always take care to **dry your hands** thoroughly before you touch anything electric. The same thing can happen if you clean a piece of electrical equipment with a wet cloth while it's still plugged in. So, as soon as you've finished using a piece of electrical equipment, dry your hands, switch it off and unplug it.
- Be extra careful with **frozen foods**. Unless you know that something can be cooked from frozen – like fish fingers or frozen peas – then always **defrost** it completely before eating or cooking it. If you can cook something from frozen, it will say so on the packet. Defrosting foods completely is especially important with **chicken** and **meat**. Otherwise you might end up with a very nasty tummy bug.

Only Cows Graze!

Have you ever spent a whole day eating rubbish? My mother once let me eat nothing but chocolate for a day. By bed-time I felt disgusting – sick, exhausted and unsatisfied. You know why? Because too much of some foods makes you feel horrible. Fatty, lovely things like sausages, chips and crisps actually slow you down. And the delicious, sugary ones – like ice-cream, chocolate and sticky buns – give you a burst of energy and then make you feel like you've climbed Everest with your feet tied together. Too much fat and sugar can make you feel lousy.

Which brings us to cows. It's not true that only cows graze. Some of us do too – eat on and off all day and never sit down to a proper meal. If you don't want to be a cow, don't graze. I suppose that's the simplest way to put it.

But it's not always that simple. There are times when you want a snack or need a snack – when you've just fallen in through the door from school, when you've exhausted yourself on the sports pitch, or when you just want some quiet time with friends. The more you eat at mealtimes, though, the less you'll even think about snacks. Meals are good. Snacks are not so good – but nice. Grazing is cow like!

Index

Aa

apples, 10
  clapple, 85
  stick-to-it, 54
  such a softy, 36
apricots: thick and sticky, 74

Bb

B & B, 116
balls first, 62
bananas: B & B, 114
  monkey mash, 34
beans, scrumptious, 101
beef: cow burglars, 106
  what is this exactly?, 109
biscuits: eight for me – none for you, 82
boof boof, 44
bread: B & B, 116
  bread and cheese please, 46
  DEB – dead easy bread, 38-9
  it's a stick up, 66-7
  roll ups, 52
breadcrumbs, 15
breakfast, 27-46
burgers: cow burglars, 106
butter, melting, 15

Cc

cakes, 16, 17
  clapple, 85
  I want it now!, 76
carrots, 10
  a sweet roast, 69
  underground, 60

cheese: bread and cheese please, 46
  no pastry pie, 105
chicken, 17
  fowl meat loaf, 64-5
  oven legs, 104
  such a sweetie, 114
chopping boards, 120
clapple, 85
corn on the cob: cracking good corn, 84
cous cous, 70-1
  green with peas, 72
  thick & sticky, 74
cow burglars, 106
cracking good corn, 84
cream cheese: FTP!, 61

Dd

DEB – dead easy bread, 38-9
dough: kneading, 15
  rolling out, 15-16

Ee

eggs, 10
  boof boof, 44
  chopped sandwich, 53
  egg in a hole, 32
  eggie piggies, 42
  fishing for eggs, 108
  hard-boiling, 14
  letuspea stew, 100
  no fry – fry up, 43
  red 'n' yellow, 92
  yum – egg whites!, 86
eight for me – none for you, 82
equipment, 19, 22-5

Ff

fab prawns, 110
fish: fishing for eggs, 108
   FTP!, 61
   some of us like fish, 94
flour, seasoned, 13
fooled you!, 115
fowl meat loaf, 64-5
FTP!, 61

Gg

garlic, 11
ginger, 11
green with peas, 72

Hh

ham: boof boof, 44
herbs, 11
hygiene, 120

Ii

I want it now!, 76
in your fingers, 75
ingredients, 10-13
it's a stick up, 66-7

Kk

knives, 120, 122

Ll

lamb: balls first, 62
leeks, 11
   underground, 60
lemon, 11
lettuce: it could be lettuce, 56
   letuspea stew, 100

Mm

Marmite: roll ups, 52
meat: browning, 13
   tenderising, 16
meat loaf, fowl, 64-5
meatballs: balls first, 62, 97
meringues: yum – egg whites, 86
monkey mash, 34
mushrooms, 11-12
   do you like mushrooms?, 98
   no fry – fry up, 43
   red 'n' yellow, 92
   scrumptious beans, 101

Nn

no fry – fry up, 43
no pastry pie, 105

Oo

one sauce, 96
onions, 12
oven legs, 104
oven temperatures, 18

Pp

parsnips: a sweet roast, 69
pastry, rolling out, 15-16
peaches, skinning, 16
pears, 10
   pears for pudding, 118
   stick-to-it, 54
   such a softy, 36
peas: green with peas, 72
   letuspea stew, 100
   peapot, 68
peppers, 12
   fab prawns, 110
   pigs and rice, 102
   red 'n' yellow, 92
pie, no pastry, 105

pigs and rice, 102
pockets, 78-80
pork: pigs and rice, 102
    in your fingers, 75
potatoes, 12
    boiled, 57
    no pastry pie, 105
    peapot, 68
    strips not chips, 81
    a sweet roast, 69
    underground, 60
    well dressed and cool, 58
pots and pans and things, 22-3
prawns, fab, 110

Rr

raspberries, 12
    fooled you!, 115
red kidney beans: scrumptious beans, 101
red 'n' yellow, 92
rice: delicious breakfast, 35
    pigs and rice, 102
roll ups, 52

Ss

safety, 120-3
salads, 12
    it could be lettuce, 56
    well dressed and cool, 58
salt, 12
sandwich, chopped, 53
sauces: one-sauce, 96
sausages: no fry – fry up, 43
scrumptious beans, 101
seasoned flour, 13
separating eggs, 10
smoked haddock: fishing for eggs, 108
spaghetti, veri quicki, 112
spare ribs: in your fingers, 75
spring onions, 13
stick-to-it, 54
strawberries, 12

strips not chips, 81
such a softy, 36
such a sweetie, 114
a sweet roast, 69

Tt

table, laying, 21
tea 4 two, 40
testing food, 16-17
thick & sticky, 74
tomatoes, 13
    chopped sandwich, 53
    no fry – fry up, 43
    no pastry pie, 105
    one-sauce, 96
    scrumptious beans, 101
    tomatoes à la Eric, 30
tuna: FTP!, 61

Uu

underground, 60

Vv

vegetables, 17
    cooking, 13-14
    a sweet roast, 69

Ww

water, 13
well dressed and cool, 58
what is this exactly?, 109
whisking, 17, 19

Yy

yum – egg whites!, 86

Zz

zest, lemon, 11

Acknowledgements

My greatest thanks to everyone who tested and tasted and talked to me – to Anna, Jake and Sarah Jauncey; to Linz, Neil and Shonagh Toulouse; to James and Sophie Dow; to Dilly Emslie; to Judy Fowlie and to Alistair Grant, Dawn Heriot and Alexander Morrison at George Heriot's School in Edinburgh.

Special thanks to my boys – to Lewis for thinking everything was gorgeous or gob-making. To Henry who traipsed the supermarket aisles with me every day for a month. To Richard for helping conceive the original idea and to our au pair George Hendrych who cooked plenty, ate everything and remained stick-thin.

Thanks also to Mary Contini whose help and advice was as brilliant as ever. To Iain Lauder at Redpath who once again created a visual feast.

Thank you to Denise Bates at Ebury Press for laughing at my jokes and for editing so wisely and sensitively. And of course, my thanks to my agent Peter Robinson for telling me when to say 'yes'.

Finally, thanks to Henry, Eliza, Josh, Connor, Jamie, Roseanna and Richard for helping out with the photographs.